Contents

Acknowledgements

First of all, I would like to thank my son-in-law, Bodie Hodge, for the massive number of hours he put into researching the content for this book and getting it ready so we could make it into what I believe is an extremely powerful publication for Christians today.

Most Christians don't know how to argue correctly and effectively in today's culture to proclaim the truth of God's Word and the gospel. Thanks, Bodie, for your vision for this topic to be dealt with and the enormous amount of work you put into enabling us to produce it. You make me look much more knowledgeable than I really am!

Secondly, I would like to thank AiG writer, speaker, and editor, Avery Foley, for her brilliant work in massaging this book to make us look good! Thanks, Avery!

—Ken Ham
General Editor

DEFENDING GOD'S EXISTENCE

KEN HAM

First printing: October 2025
Second printing: February 2026

Master Books, P.O. Box 726, Green Forest, AR 72638
Master Books® is a division of the New Leaf Publishing Group, LLC.

ISBN: 978-1-68344-382-7
ISBN: 978-1-61458-900-6 (digital)
Library of Congress Control Number: 2025931452

Cover by Left Coast Designs

Please consider requesting that a copy of this volume be purchased by your local library system.

Printed in the United States of America

Please visit our website for other great titles:
www.masterbooks.com

For information regarding promotional opportunities, please contact the publicity department at pr@nlpg.com.

Foreword

Does God really exist?

This question has massive implications. If God doesn't exist, we must be products of naturalistic evolution over millions of years. We're just animals, no different and of no more inherent value than slugs, baboons, or bananas. There is no ultimate purpose or meaning to life and no hope beyond the grave because when you're dead, that's it, you're dead. There is no absolute right or wrong, no justice, and no true accountability because we're nothing but bags of chemicals and chemicals aren't responsible for any of the consequences of their reactions.

That's a pretty bleak picture and few atheists or skeptics live like it's true. They generally care about their own lives, and those of their families, friends, and communities. They usually believe strongly about right and wrong, justice, and even meaning and purpose. But it's all without foundation because if there really is no God…it all means nothing. Everything ends in nothingness; no one will remember they were ever here.

What a depressing way to start a book! But that is what is at stake when you ask the question, "Does God exist?" You aren't just asking, "Is there an eternal being somewhere out in the universe?" You're really asking:

- Is there meaning and purpose to my life?
- Am I more than just an animal and a chemical reaction?
- Is there life after death?
- Do right and wrong really exist?
- Why am I here?

And the good news—the best news—is that atheists are utterly, completely, and foolishly wrong. Their worldview simply doesn't stand up to scrutiny (I'm getting ahead of myself as we will get to those arguments soon). The only answer to the question that makes sense of what we observe is yes, God exists; specifically the God of the Bible exists.

If you don't yet know this God, whether you're an atheist, a skeptic, or just curious, I pray you will read this book and feel convicted about your beliefs. That you will see the inconsistency of all other religious beliefs expect biblical Christianity. And, ultimately, that you will come to know Jesus Christ, the God-man, as your Lord and Savior.

Giving up on atheism, unbelief, or even curiosity may feel like giving up control over your life (and it is—when you become a Christian, you give your life over to the God of the universe, to become His servant, walking in obedience to Him) but, as a life-long follower of Christ, I can promise you: it's worth it. He's worth it all.

God exists; He loves you; He died and rose again for you; and He's promised there is eternity waiting you after your last breath. And it's either with Him in heaven or without Him in hell. The stakes couldn't be higher, but God has made it obvious to all that He exists because He wants everyone—you included—to come to repentance.

So let's get started.

Ken Ham
CEO Answers in Genesis, Creation Museum, and Ark Encounter

Introduction: The Existence of God

Why don't I use the classical arguments for the existence of God?

I've been speaking and writing on apologetics for 50 years but if you've followed my ministry for any length of time, you may have noticed I rarely, if ever, use the classical arguments for the existence of God. These are arguments such as first cause, design in nature, the ontological argument, or the teleological argument. Why not?

It's not because these arguments are never effective. They sometimes are. Just recently the co-founder of Wikipedia, Larry Sanger, detailed his testimony of coming to saving faith in Christ and these classical arguments featured prominently. So, they can be effective at times (and praise God for that—He's the one who saves, not our clever arguments). Why then don't I use them?

I don't use them largely because you can only take them so far. At some point near the end of the argument, there's always a gigantic leap of logic to say the God whose existence you've logically proved was and is the "God of the Bible." You see, classical arguments are not arguments specifically for the God of the Bible but rather for a "generic god" or a generic concept of a "deity."

Christian apologists (defenders of the Christian faith) for more than a thousand years used these classical methods. But not just Christians—*non-Christians* also used these methods when arguing for their alleged God/god(s). In fact, even the great ancient Greek philosopher *Aristotle* used one of these classical methods to argue for a "god" against the backdrop of polytheism (i.e., "many gods").

Here's the point: Classical arguments for the existence of *a god* do *not* necessarily argue for the biblical God. That is, these arguments have been used to argue for *any alleged* "god"—such as Zeus, Thor, Allah, the Great Spirit, Saturn, Baal, or any other false god—with the supposed goal of simply trying to convince someone to not be an "atheist."

Back in the 1980's there was an American atheist activist and free-thought intellectual named *Dr. Gordon Stein* who was "wreaking havoc" on Christians. He published books that challenged the existence of God by dismantling these classical methods. He realized there were significant logical problems with them and simply capitalized on those weaknesses.

He would debate Christians and often leave them looking very foolish. That was until 1985 when he debated a Christian philosopher and pastor, *Dr. Greg Bahnsen at the University of California, Irvine on atheism vs. theism.* Bahnsen, unlike many other Christians, *opposed* the typical use of the classical arguments as he also saw the problems with them. Instead, he used the *transcendental* argument in the famous "Great Debate" (which I strongly recommend every Christian listen to at least once!).

Dr. Stein was stopped dead in his tracks as Bahnsen forced him to account for the inconsistencies of his own atheistic worldview and, without the classical arguments to rip apart, *his argument* was left in ashes and he looked foolish. He began to completely stumble over his responses to Bahnsen in the debate. As a result, his fame as arguably one of the most famous atheists (even on par with famed atheist *Dr. Richard Dawkins*) was washed away. So much so that most atheists today don't even remember his name!

After this debate, Greg Bahnsen informally earned the title, "The Man Most Feared by Atheists." Of course, the *Man* that atheists should fear is the God-man—Jesus Christ—who Bahnsen was defending.

So… what are *"apologetics," "philosophy,"* and *"logic"*? How do they intertwine? Why do these *classical arguments for the existence of God* fall short? What is the *transcendental argument for the existence of God* (often abbreviated simply as "TAG"), and why is it so powerful? We'll explore all those questions, and more, throughout this book.

As you read, there will likely be times you'll say something like, "Oh, that is so obvious" or "I understand that easily," but there will surely be places where you suddenly realize how deep the "ocean of philosophy" can get. You may even say, "Do I want to keep reading because this seems like it is way over my head?"

When you hit these points, I want to encourage you to just keep on reading. As we go, I'll reiterate certain teachings and points in multiple ways, at multiple depths, and with multiple illustrations, so just keep going—I promise by the end of the book, you'll get it.

When you get to those points where you have to read some things (at least) twice, don't let that bother you. When it comes to philosophy, sometimes I've had to read things 2 or 3 (or 4 or 5 times!) to even somewhat grasp it. I don't want to burden you with having to read things over and over, so I'm trying to be mindful of that when writing.

As you take this journey into philosophy and apologetics, enjoy it and remember that it's not merely to gain more "head knowledge"—it's to better defend the existence of our Savior, Jesus Christ, to a world that desperately needs to know that He is who He says He is: the eternal God who alone can save.

> *Where is the wise? Where is the scribe? Where is the disputer of this age? Has not God made foolish the wisdom of this world?* (1 Corinthians 1:20)

Apologetics – What Is It?

But sanctify the Lord God in your hearts, and always be ready to give a defense (apologia) to everyone who asks you a reason for the hope that is in you, with meekness and fear. (1 Peter 3:15)

What Is Apologetics and What Is Its Purpose?

The phrase translated "to give a defense" or sometimes "give an answer" in 1 Peter 3:15 comes from the Greek word *apologia (ἀπολογία)*, which literally means, "a reasoned defense" (or a "verbal defense," like in a court of law). (Note, it does *not* mean to *apologize*, even though the two words sound similar!). Simply put, it means to give *a logical defense of the Christian faith.*

Apologetics is a vital branch of Christianity that defends the authority of the Bible, the character of God, and Christianity as a whole. When we do apologetics, we are using the Bible as an offensive spiritual "weapon" (e.g., like a sword) against all other worldviews and opposition to Christianity. Apologetics is essential when discussing the existence of the biblical God—which is one of the foremost discussions in general apologetics.

As believers in our modern era, we need to be equipped with *general apologetics* to be able to defend general theology, miracles, the reliability of biblical manuscripts, the Resurrection, and the existence of God. General apologetics is the focus of this book.

But, in the times we live in where Genesis 1–11 (the foundational history God has given us that forms the basis for our worldview) is the most attacked portion of Scripture, we also need to be equipped with *creation apologetics. Why? Well, if you start arguing for God's existence with a skeptic, I guarantee it won't take long before you'll be dealing with questions about evolution, millions of years, the global Flood, racism, LGBTQ issues, abortion, death and suffering,* and other attacks surrounding Genesis 1–11.[1]

Apologetics is an exciting area of study to help strengthen our faith as believers, defend Christianity, and cause unbelievers to question the shaky foundation of their own worldview. But please don't misunderstand this important point: Apologetics is *not* a tool to make people believe in Christ. The Bible is clear that "faith comes by hearing and hearing by the Word of God" (Romans 10:17[2]) and "no one can say that Jesus is Lord except by the Holy Spirit" (1 Corinthians 12:3[3]). I compare apologetics to Jesus raising Lazarus from the dead.[4] Unbelievers are dead inside; they cannot save themselves. When Jesus raised Lazarus He commanded those standing around to move the stone away from the tomb. Jesus is all-powerful. He could have commanded the stone to move and it would've obeyed! But Jesus had Lazarus' family and friends do what they could do—move the stone (e.g. present apologetics and the gospel)—and Jesus did what only He can do: raised the dead!

So, while they can't save, prayerful apologetics can help "move the stones" from skeptical hearts as we point to God's Word and the gospel, showing unbelievers that the Bible is true, and therefore the gospel is also true.

Apologetics can also *reinforce* the faith of believers, encouraging them to stand more boldly on the authority of God's Word in every area, and increase their confidence in evangelism as they now have answers to the skeptical questions raised against God's authority.

1. You can find resources to equip you on creation apologetics at AnswersinGenesis.org.
2. So then faith comes by hearing, and hearing by the word of God. (Romans 10:17)
3. Therefore I make known to you that no one speaking by the Spirit of God calls Jesus accursed, and no one can say that Jesus is Lord except by the Holy Spirit. (1 Corinthians 12:3)
4. Read the full account of Lazarus in John 11.

Apologetics Are Two Pronged: Offense and Defense

According to 1 Peter 3:15 every Christian must have a defensive apologetic. But many other passages of Scripture command us, as Christians, to also have an *offense*.

Imagine this: you're playing a game but your team is only ever allowed to play defense, never offense. Would you win the game? Not a chance! At best, if your defense was nearly perfect, you could tie (assuming the other team doesn't forfeit, of course!). It's the same in apologetics, you need defense to show why our worldview is the right one, and offense to show why the unbeliever's worldview is the wrong one.

The Bible is described as a *sword*, and a sword is obviously used for both defense *and* offense in battle.

> *For the word of God is living and powerful, and sharper than any two-edged sword, piercing even to the division of soul and spirit, and of joints and marrow, and is a discerner of the thoughts and intents of the heart.* (Hebrews 4:12)

The Bible also describes believers as have spiritual "weapons of our warfare:"

> *For the weapons of our warfare are not carnal but mighty in God for pulling down strongholds, casting down arguments and every high thing that exalts itself against the knowledge of God, bringing every thought into captivity to the obedience of Christ, and being ready to punish all disobedience when your obedience is fulfilled.* (2 Corinthians 10:4–6)

The ESV puts verse 5 this way: "*We destroy arguments and every lofty opinion raised against the knowledge of God, and take every thought captive to obey Christ.*" In other words, when under attack, the Christian has two primary defenses available: defend (answer) and/or disarm (go on the offense). You'll need both of these "basics of Christian apologetics" when sharing the gospel with an unbeliever.

It's like this: if someone comes at you with a knife, you can defend yourself by blocking or moving out of the way every time the attacker strikes. Or the better option, if possible, is to *disarm* your opponent by taking away the knife altogether.

In apologetics, you can defend by answering all the questions presented by the unbeliever, trying to shoot down every attack. Or you can *disarm* the unbeliever completely by refuting the very basis of their philosophical attacks, pointing out that they have a faulty starting point for their worldview. In other words, exposing the reality that they have no foundation whatsoever for their beliefs in the first place. Of course, all this should be done with meekness and fear (i.e., gentleness and respect) as the last part of 1 Peter 3:15 instructs us.

As a practical example, an evolutionist once mockingly said to me that he couldn't believe that Bible believers (like me) actually believe that all the people in the world came from just two people, Adam and Eve. I had two choices in how to respond: one, I could've scientifically defended this biblical truth, pointing, for example, to new finds in genetics. But he wasn't looking for answers—he was just mocking me. So I went on the offensive and took my second option: I responded that I couldn't understand how people holding to his (evolutionary) worldview believe all the people in the world came from a *rock*.[5] Then I brought in the defensive: I told him we observe people come from people all the time but we don't see people come from rocks.[6]

In this apologetic, I was highlighting that he hadn't even considered the absurdity of his own position, where the biblical position actually does make sense. Having people descend from Adam and Eve is actually quite logical.

The Care of the Apologist

The Bible commands us, as Christians, to be prepared to give a reasoned defense of the faith but 1 Peter 3:15 also makes it clear that our defense of the faith must start with setting apart Christ as Lord in our hearts, and acting with *gentleness and respect*. (These two points are critically important when defending the Christian faith, so don't miss this!)

---

5. Yes, you read that correctly. Evolutionists really do believe we owe our existence to rocks. (In other words, our ancestors were rocks!) For example, see this article: https://www.science.org/content/article/you-owe-your-life-rock.
6. Of course, the Bible does say that the first man (Adam) was formed by God from the "dust of the ground" (Genesis 2:7), so the point is not that it's impossible for humans to come from "rocks." Rather, the point here is that only the biblical worldview actually provides a ***logical basis*** for our existence—that we all descend from Adam (Acts 17:26). Whereas the evolutionist cannot even make sense of the question of where we came from, given his faulty worldview—failing to realize the inconsistency in his argument and the absurdity of his beliefs.

Far too often, Christians obtain a few answers and immediately think they are ready to "force" those answers on to people so they can beat their opponent. But that's not the right attitude! Instead, apologetics isn't about "forcing" anything on anyone. It's about sharing the gospel with gentleness and respect so that "God perhaps will grant them repentance, so that they may know the truth, and that they may come to their senses and escape the snare of the devil" (2 Timothy 2:25b, 26a). We need to show the same grace, mercy, patience, and love that the Lord showed to us.

This is why apologetics should always be used in conjunction with the *Gospel* (Matthew 28:18–20[7]; Mark 16:15[8]); in other words, don't do apologetics for the sake of trying to win an argument, but do it for the sake of the Gospel (Good News) of Jesus Christ.

Consider another pertinent passage related to apologetics:

> *If anyone teaches otherwise and does not consent to wholesome words, even the words of our Lord Jesus Christ, and to the doctrine which accords with godliness, he is proud, knowing nothing, but is obsessed with disputes and arguments over words, from which come envy, strife, reviling, evil suspicions, useless wranglings of men of corrupt minds and destitute of the truth, who suppose that godliness is a means of gain. From such withdraw yourself.* (1 Timothy 6:3–5)

We must also use discernment when discussing the things of God. Many apologists get caught up debating one person (who refuses to be corrected) much longer than they should (I often see this in the comment section of my social media pages!), sometimes over the course of years. Consider what the Scriptures say about this:

> *But avoid foolish disputes, genealogies, contentions, and strivings about the law; for they are unprofitable and useless. Reject a divisive man after the first and second admonition, knowing that such a person is warped and sinning, being self-condemned.* (Titus 3:9–11)

---

7. And Jesus came and spoke to them, saying, "All authority has been given to Me in heaven and on earth. Go therefore and make disciples of all the nations, baptizing them in the name of the Father and of the Son and of the Holy Spirit, teaching them to observe all things that I have commanded you; and lo, I am with you always, even to the end of the age." Amen. (Matthew 28:18–20)
8. And He said to them, "Go into all the world and preach the gospel to every creature." (Mark 16:15)

Do not give what is holy to the dogs; nor cast your pearls before swine, lest they trample them under their feet, and turn and tear you in pieces. (Matthew 7:6)

And whoever will not receive you, when you go out of that city, shake off the very dust from your feet as a testimony against them. (Luke 9:5)

In other words, when it becomes obvious that someone is not willing to learn, shows no signs of change, or does not even consider they could be wrong, do not continue wasting time with them (on the account of their hard hearts). Simply move on and seek more fruitful evangelism with others who are willing to listen. But even when we must move on, we can continue to pray for that person, that God would someday soften their hard heart—and when that begins to happen, we're ready with apologetics and the gospel again!

Some Christians (falsely) think that the Bible commands us to give an answer back to those people who are arguing against the Christian faith repeatedly (for years even) because of 1 Peter 3:15. But it doesn't say to always give an answer, but always "be *prepared* to give an answer" (NIV).

Again, it's important for Christians to recognize the times to give answers and the times to refrain (Titus 3:9–10[9]). For example, when people fail to listen [even professing Christians] (2 Peter 2:3[10]) and you can discern that they obviously do not want to be instructed (Proverbs 1:7[11]), or when their purpose is to be divisive (Romans 16:17[12]), then it is time to move on.

Practical Apologetics

When defending the faith, the apologist should always present the Christian worldview from the starting point of the Bible (Mark 16:15[13]; Proverbs 26:4[14]). This means we start with the authority of God's Word. That Christian worldview includes, but is not limited to:

9. But avoid foolish disputes, genealogies, contentions, and strivings about the law; for they are unprofitable and useless. Reject a divisive man after the first and second admonition. (Titus 3:9–10)
10. By covetousness they will exploit you with deceptive words; for a long time their judgment has not been idle, and their destruction does not slumber. (2 Peter 2:3)
11. The fear of the LORD is the beginning of knowledge, But fools despise wisdom and instruction. (Proverbs 1:7)
12. Now I urge you, brethren, note those who cause divisions and offenses, contrary to the doctrine which you learned, and avoid them. (Romans 16:17)
13. Ibid. Ref. 8.
14. Do not answer a fool according to his folly, Lest you also be like him. (Proverbs 26:4)

1 Creation week was a period of six ordinary 24-hour days. How can one stand on the authority of Scripture and then question the history the Bible presents to us? If Genesis is not true, then why is the rest of the Bible true? By the way, an all-powerful God creating in six days and resting on seventh day as a basis for our work week (Exodus 20:11[15]) is all too easy a task for Him.

2 Man was made in the image of God (Genesis 1:27[16]). Man is not the product of random chemical reactions over millions of years. Therefore, man is not an evolved animal; he is a unique creation of God and therefore human life has value. (According to atheism, naturalism, and humanism, we just evolved and therefore have no more inherent value than any other form of matter, such as cats, dogs, cockroaches, trees, grass, or dirt.)

3 God created a perfect world where there was no death, suffering, or disease (Genesis 1:31[17]; Deuteronomy 32:4[18]). Man's sin brought death, suffering, animal carnivory,[19] "thorns and thistles,"[20] and corruption to this perfect world (Genesis 3). The Bible describes death as an "enemy" (1 Corinthians 15:26[21]) and our fallen word as groaning because of sin.[22] The Fall of mankind explains both the beauty and ugliness of this world and the existence of death and suffering and therefore the need for a Savior, Jesus Christ, and the need for a new heavens and new earth where there will be no more death or suffering (Revelation 21:4[23]).

---

15. For in six days the LORD made the heavens and the earth, the sea, and all that is in them, and rested the seventh day. Therefore the LORD blessed the Sabbath day and hallowed it. (Exodus 20:11)
16. So God created man in His own image; in the image of God He created him; male and female He created them. (Genesis 1:27)
17. Then God saw everything that He had made, and indeed it was very good. So the evening and the morning were the sixth day. (Genesis 1:31)
18. He is the Rock, His work is perfect; For all His ways are justice, A God of truth and without injustice; Righteous and upright is He. (Deuteronomy 32:4)
19. And God said, "See, I have given you every herb that yields seed which is on the face of all the earth, and every tree whose fruit yields seed; to you it shall be for food. Also, to every beast of the earth, to every bird of the air, and to everything that creeps on the earth, in which there is life, I have given every green herb for food"; and it was so. (Genesis 1:29–30)
20. Then to Adam He said, "Because you have heeded the voice of your wife, and have eaten from the tree of which I commanded you, saying, 'You shall not eat of it': "Cursed is the ground for your sake; In toil you shall eat of it, All the days of your life. Both thorns and thistles it shall bring forth for you."" (Genesis 3:17–18a)
21. The last enemy that will be destroyed is death. (1 Corinthians 15:26)
22. For we know that the whole creation groans and labors with birth pangs together until now. (Romans 8:22)
23. And God will wipe away every tear from their eyes; there shall be no more death, nor sorrow, nor crying. There shall be no more pain, for the former things have passed away. (Revelation 21:4)

4 The global Flood of Noah's day (Genesis 6–9) explains why we have rock layers filled with fossils. This also shows that God, who is a righteous judge, does judge sin, but also, by His mercy, sends a means of salvation (i.e., the ark).

5 The dispersion of peoples at the Tower of Babel (Genesis 11) explains the existence of people groups with minor physical variations and why we speak different languages, even though we are one race, all sinners, and all in need of a Savior.

6 Moses and the Law gives us the standard to define what sin is (as it reigned from the time of Adam) and shows how we fall short of meeting that perfect standard. It relates to how Christ fulfilled the law on behalf of guilty sinners and offers grace to those who repent and trust in Him.

7 Christ and His work on the Cross is the only means of salvation. When Christ, the God-man, died on the cross, He paid the penalty of death we deserve for us. Then He rose from the grave, conquering sin and death. He now offers the free gift of salvation to those who repent (turn from their sin) and believe in Jesus Christ and His death and resurrection.

8 Jesus will someday return and create a new heavens and a new earth to fulfill everything that God has promised. (Christians look forward to this coming day when there will be no more death or suffering for all of eternity.)

Many times, when we present a Christian worldview to the unbeliever, it involves clearing up misconceptions about Christianity. A few examples are:

1 God is one God who is triune (three persons – Father, Son, and the Holy Spirit – each person is fully God, equal in glory, and coeternal), not three separate "gods."

2 Christianity is based on the 66 infallible, inerrant, authoritative, and sufficient books of the Bible, given to us by God (the Holy Spirit is the ultimate author of Scripture who used ordinary, sinful men, who often fail to live up to the standards in the Bible, to pen the words).

3 God created the world perfect, not the way it is today. It has been subjected to death and decay due to man's sin (Genesis 1:31[24], Deuteronomy 32:4[25], Genesis 3, Romans 8). Death and suffering are a result of sin, but God stepped into history as Jesus Christ the God-man to die in place of sinners and save them from sin and death.

24. Ibid. Ref. 17.
25. Ibid. Ref. 18.

We must also realize that, in a sin-cursed and broken world, all unbelievers ultimately start their thinking based on man's (fallible) word instead God's (infallible) Word (e.g., see Ephesians 4:17–18,[26] 1 Corinthians 1:21,[27] 1 Corinthians 2:14,[28] 1 Corinthians 3:19,[29] Colossians 2:8,[30] Romans 1:18–28). This foundation of man's word can take a variety of forms—literally their own thinking, the general thinking of our culture, another "holy book," and so on—but all unbelievers ultimately reject God's perfect Word and therefore have no foundation but human reasoning. I've often described it this way: there's really only two religions, in an ultimate sense—God's and not God's. Either you start with the one true God and His Word, or you're by default starting with man's word. There's no other option!

Now, in order to effectively expose the foolishness of a false worldview, we must understand the way unbelievers think. This means you need to know as much as possible about the other person's professed worldview so that you can refute it *biblically* and *logically* (with gentleness and respect, of course). Now, you don't need to completely master every other religious belief system—a basic and foundational knowledge is great but even that can be difficult. So, when you're witnessing, learn as must as possible about the other person's worldview by asking the person questions. Most people are happy to discuss what they believe and that lets you know exactly what that specific person actually believes.

As you ask questions and discover that person's specific beliefs, you can then go on the offensive, doing an internal critique of the unbeliever's worldview (Proverbs 26:5[31], 2 Timothy 2:25[32]). Point out where they are being arbitrary, inconsistent, where their worldview's ultimate conclusion

26. This I say, therefore, and testify in the Lord, that you should no longer walk as the rest of the Gentiles walk, in the futility of their mind, having their understanding darkened, being alienated from the life of God, because of the ignorance that is in them, because of the blindness of their heart. (Ephesians 4:17-18)
27. For since, in the wisdom of God, the world through wisdom did not know God, it pleased God through the foolishness of the message preached to save those who believe. (1 Corinthians 1:21)
28. But the natural man does not receive the things of the Spirit of God, for they are foolishness to him; nor can he know them, because they are spiritually discerned. (1 Corinthians 2:14)
29. For the wisdom of this world is foolishness with God. For it is written, "He catches the wise in their own craftiness." (1 Corinthians 3:19)
30. Beware lest anyone cheat you through philosophy and empty deceit, according to the tradition of men, according to the basic principles of the world, and not according to Christ. (Colossians 2:8)
31. Answer a fool according to his folly, Lest he be wise in his own eyes. (Proverbs 26:5)
32. In humility correcting those who are in opposition, if God perhaps will grant them repentance, so that they may know the truth. (2 Timothy 2:25)

leads (e.g., reduced to absurdity), and even cases where they borrow from the Bible.[33] The following chapter discusses how to refute a belief system in more detail.

And, never forget the ultimate goal—the gospel! As you defend and go on the offense, continually point people to God's Word as the absolute truth and present the Gospel. Many times this can be done when presenting the Christian worldview. But make sure the gospel is "front and center" in apologetics as the Gospel of Jesus Christ is of utmost importance.

In other words, your apologetic should work together with the gospel. This is important because we, as Christians, can often spend *way* too much time on apologetics during our witnessing encounters that we forget the gospel! Simply put, in our defense of the faith, our goal should always be to glorify God and lead people to the cross, and if we fail to do those two things, then we've ultimately failed in our apologetic!

Conclusion

When arguing for the existence of the biblical God, remember these key points: We do this for the sake of the gospel and the authority of the Bible. We do this with gentleness and respect. Unbelievers are *not* the enemy; the enemy is the false worldview that has taken them "captive" (2 Timothy 2:24-26,[34] Colossians 2:8,[35] 2 Corinthians 10:4–5[36]). Whether they realize it or not, unbelievers are made in the image of God and they are your relative—and ultimately in need of Jesus Christ to be saved.

---

33. For more on these topics please consult Dr. Greg Bahnsen's book *Always Ready* or Dr. Jason Lisle's book *The Ultimate Proof of Creation*.
34. And a servant of the Lord must not quarrel but be gentle to all, able to teach, patient, in humility correcting those who are in opposition, if God perhaps will grant them repentance, so that they may know the truth, and that they may come to their senses and escape the snare of the devil, having been taken captive by him to do his will. (2 Timothy 2:24–26)
35. Ibid. Ref. 30.
36. For the weapons of our warfare are not carnal but mighty in God for pulling down strongholds, casting down arguments and every high thing that exalts itself against the knowledge of God, bringing every thought into captivity to the obedience of Christ. (2 Corinthians 10:4–5)

How to Refute (Disprove) Something

In Contradiction with the 66 Books of the Bible

There are so many beliefs, worldviews, and opinions out there. How can we tell if something is true or false? Simple: we compare it against the Bible. If it is in disagreement with God and the 66 books of His Word, then it is wrong.

Yes, it's really that simple: If something contradicts God's Word, then that argument, worldview, or position is *false.*

You see, the God of the Bible is all-knowing, eternal, and never lies. He is the source and standard of truth. Therefore He is the only One who is *always* right on all matters to which He speaks. He alone is the absolute authority as to whether something is right or wrong.

Actually, as we'll see, the concepts of right, wrong, true, false, correct, and incorrect are only possible because the biblical God exists and has given us His Word. Because God is the standard for these things, He defines them.

Obviously not everyone believes this. But for those who object, by what *authority* do they object? Or by what *standard* can they complain about anything at all? They are mere creatures; they are not all-knowing, are not eternal, do not have all authority, and cannot even remotely begin to compete with God who created and upholds all things in existence (Colossians 1:16–17[1]).

When a creature objects to the Creator, their objection is merely *arbitrary* (there is no basis or power behind their arguments) because they are a *lesser authority* than God. Obviously, finite human reasoning is a lower standard than the infinite Word of God. Thus, any objection to God is a *faulty appeal to authority* fallacy. (This is also called a *false authority fallacy* or *misplaced authority fallacy*.) When you spot this fallacy—in other words, when someone objects to the authority of God and His Word—you know the argument is fallacious and illogical right from the start.

When you are speaking with someone and he or she uses an argument, takes a position, espouses a worldview, has an objection, or has any sort of knowledge claim at all that is in opposition to the clear teachings of the Bible, then understand it is by necessity refuted and proved false—they just don't know it yet!—and the Bible remains true, accurate, and the standard for correct logical reasoning.

AIP Argument Analysis Checklist

Many people will not listen if you point out that they've committed a faulty appeal to authority fallacy—after all, most people do think they're a pretty good authority! It's part of our sin nature to want to be our own gods and decide truth for ourselves. So that's where you disprove their worldview or argument by refuting it *within* its own story, own worldview, or own argument. In other words, you show their standard to be what it is: a faulty one.

With this technique, you're doing an internal critique of their argument by asking three questions:

1. For by Him all things were created that are in heaven and that are on earth, visible and invisible, whether thrones or dominions or principalities or powers. All things were created through Him and for Him. And He is before all things, and in Him all things consist. (Colossians 1:16–17)

- Is it *Arbitrary*?
- Is it *Inconsistent*?
- Does it violate the *Preconditions of Intelligibility*?

You can think of this as "the AIP checklist" (**A**rbitrary, **I**nconsistent, and **P**reconditions). You won't formally stop the person speaking and verbally run each argument through this checklist, but keep this "AIP test" in the back of your mind as you're listening (or reading) to critique the unbeliever's arguments.

Oh, and don't let the "fancy" philosophical terms scare you. I'll define them as we go along with the purpose of using them to look for errors in reasoning to disprove something from its own story.

Is It Arbitrary?

The first stop on our AIP checklist is the question, "Is it arbitrary?" Philosophically (and biblically speaking), arbitrariness is bad; it's a "fatal flaw" in logical reasoning. If something is arbitrary, it simply means there is nothing of substance behind the argument. Rather, the argument is based on conjectures, opinions, bias, or relativistic thinking. None of these carry any weight because there is no authority behind the argument. For any argument or debate to be rational and logical, no one can merely assert a claim—with no justification for it—and then expect others to accept that claim. To do so is arbitrary and renders the argument meaningless.

That's Just Conjecture

Back in the 1970's, I was a science teacher in a public high school in the country town of Dalby, Australia, in Queensland. The students in my first science class found out I was a Christian and immediately challenged me, "Sir, we saw you're a Christian—how can you be a Christian when we know the Bible isn't true?" When I asked for their reasons why the Bible isn't true, one student responded with, "Noah couldn't get all those animals on the ark!" When I asked him how big the ark was or how many animals Noah needed to take on board, he said he didn't know.

This student's objection fails the AIP checklist because it's just a conjecture (specifically, it's what's called an *ignorant conjecture* because he hadn't done any research before making his claim!) A conjecture is arbitrary because it has no real weight behind the belief, he was just repeating some talking point he'd heard somewhere without knowing any details or facts.[2] This happens often (especially on the internet and social media!).

Mere Opinion

I was on a radio talk program once when a caller asked the common question, "Where did Cain get his wife?" I answered saying everyone was descended from the first two people, Adam and Eve, so Cain's wife must have been his sister (or possibly a niece). These close intermarriages are common in Genesis (Abraham married his half sister, Sarah, for example). God then ends close marriages when He gives the Law to Moses 2,500 years later. Well, the next caller identified himself as an atheist and objected, "If you believe that, it's incest and it's immoral."

But why? (We could say, "by what standard?") This atheist is asserting nothing but his own mere opinion because, in his worldview, there is no foundation for morality. He's just giving his opinion and mere opinions are arbitrary and have no weight behind their claims.[3] This argument fails the first stop on the AIP checklist too.

Your Bias Is Showing

Through the years I've heard the claim that "creationists can't be real scientists" over and over again. It doesn't matter how many times scientists who believe the Bible publish in academic journals or follow the scientific method and make discoveries, their work is dismissed outright because of bias and prejudice.

For example, Harvard-trained biologist Dr. Nathaniel Jeanson has published ground-breaking research in genetics—research that has been confirmed by observational science.[4] And yet when he sent his work to evolutionists for

2. Please note that making an ignorant conjecture does not mean making a reasonable prediction based on available data (that's a different discussion). Rather, when people make ignorant conjectures, it simply means they failed to use information that is publicly/widely available.
3. To be clear, being arbitrary means to merely assume something to be true, assert that belief with no justification for it at all, and expect the other party to just accept it. And so, when people (like evolutionists) give bad reasons for their claims, they're not being arbitrary. Rather, it's a bad reason that must be exposed as being inconsistent and/or a violation of the *preconditions of intelligibility*.
4. See *Replacing Darwin, Traced,* and *They Had Names.*

critical review, most didn't respond, one flatly refused to even look at it, and the one person who agreed to debate Dr. Jeanson clearly hadn't even read the book!

This "creationists can't be real scientists" argument fails the AIP test because of the person's bias. It is arbitrary to reject someone simply based on an unargued *bias* or *prejudice.*

All Things Relative

I've often heard those in the LGBTQ lobby argue they just want tolerance for all views. But when I state the biblical view of one man and one woman for life, they say they can't allow for that view! They can allow for a variety of views (except the view that excludes their view!) because their morality is based on relativism. Like so many today, they believe individual truth is different for different people and so we should be open to everything (i.e. everyone's truth—except the Bible, of course!).

This is an example of an arbitrary assertion based on *relativism*. There is no real meat behind their assertions, and so it is arbitrary.

In summary, arbitrariness can be generally broken into four common categories:

1	*Ignorant Conjecture*
2	*Mere Opinion*
3	*Unargued Bias*
4	*Relativism*

Note: It's perfectly okay if you don't remember these exact names! What's important is to be able to recognize and simply (and gently) point out when someone's argument is based on arbitrariness.

Is It Inconsistent?

The next stop on our AIP checklist is, "Is it inconsistent?" If someone is being inconsistent in his/her argument (i.e., having contrary beliefs), they are being illogical. Again, just like with arbitrariness, philosophically (and biblically speaking), *inconsistency* is bad, another "fatal flaw" in logical reasoning. No one is allowed to be inconsistent in his/her argument or worldview and still have a "good" argument.

The most obvious way to show someone is being inconsistent is to find ***logical fallacies***. These are common errors in reasoning.

Many logical fallacies have names and have been documented for thousands of years. Some still use ancient Latin names for instance, even though we do have modern English names for them too! (The following chapter gives you a breakdown of many of the common logical fallacies.)

Sadly, most people (including many Christians) were never taught basic logic in school, which is why, many times, logic just "goes out the window" when discussing worldviews. But it's very beneficial for Christians to learn to at least spot the major logical fallacies when defending the faith.

Another way to look for inconsistency is by ***reducing the argument to absurdity*** *by where it leads*. (The fancy name in Latin is *Reductio Ad Absurdum*.) To do this, simply ask yourself, if the argument is true, what are the consequences? In other words, take the argument to its logical conclusion. If it leads to something crazy or absurd, then it is inconsistent, and thus it is false.

Consider the popular mantra, "love is love." When we take this idea that someone's feelings of "love" (whatever "love" means) determine morality to its logical conclusion, we must allow for "consenting" pederasty and pedophilia, adultery, polygamy, polyandry, polyamory, and any other sexual behavior because, well, "love is love!" But few in our society want to go that far! And yet that's the logical conclusion to that argument.

Another way to show inconsistency is through behavior. If someone preaches one thing and lives another way, that shows a ***behavioral inconsistency***. It shows they really don't believe what they claim to believe.[5]

When I debated Bill Nye, TV's "Science Guy," at the Creation Museum in 2014 and again at the Ark Encounter in 2016 (an informal debate as we

5. Note this kind of inconsistency doesn't necessarily mean their worldview is false. Many professing Christians have said the right beliefs, but behind-the-scenes they are not living by the Bible's standard. That doesn't make the Bible false, it simply makes the person inconsistent with the truth. Be ready to answer this objection! Actually, it makes a great "springboard" for the gospel because the Bible explains this inconsistency—sin! Show the unbeliever where sin (including hypocrisy) came from, our need for a Savior to save us from sin, and our hope of the new creation where there will be no more sin, including lying or hypocrisy.

walked through the life-size Ark) he made it clear he was an atheist who believed there is no real meaning or purpose to life. And yet he frequently talks about the meaning of life being "the wonder of discovery." When I pushed him on this point, that in his worldview everything is ultimately meaningless—when you're dead you're dead, nothing matters—he just kept going back to the wonder of discovery. In other words, he didn't really believe his own atheistic worldview. He believed there was meaning even though his worldview can't account of it.

Simply put, when your actions disagree with your words, it shows this type of inconsistency.

The final type of inconsistency is ***presuppositional tension***. Don't let the "fancy" words scare you! This is simply where you look at the basis for your argument to see if there is consistency for it. It's like the opposite version of *Reductio Ad Absurdum*. Instead of looking at the logical conclusion of a given argument or worldview and seeing if it leads to absurdity, it looks at potential inconsistencies right up front to see if the *foundation* of the worldview in question is actually consistent with stated initial beliefs. This tension can show a contradiction, and thus expose the worldview as fallacious.

Ever heard someone say, "there are no absolutes"? Well, are they absolutely sure about that? The foundation of this statement isn't consistent with the stated belief. Another example is a materialist arguing for his materialistic worldview. Do you spot the tension in the materialist's worldview? If his materialism is correct, then truth can't exist because truth isn't material. This is *contradictory* to his stated belief.

Note that this last form of inconsistency can have some crossover with the "P" in our AIP checklist, as you'll see in a moment. But I include it here because I want you to realize that sometimes an argument can be wrong in *more than one way*. For instance, sometimes people commit a logical fallacy and are arbitrary at the same time. Or sometimes people commit multiple logical fallacies at the same time! Don't feel like you have to point them all out, every time (that will probably just make you seem arrogant and condescending!). Just pick one or two of the most obvious examples and use those.

In summary, inconsistency (errors) in reasoning can be generally broken into four common categories:

1	*Logical Fallacies*
2	*Reduced to Absurdity*
3	*Behavioral Inconsistencies*
4	*Presuppositional Tension*

Again, it's totally fine if you don't remember these names! The important takeaway here is you need to be able to simply (and gently) point out when someone is being inconsistent in his/her argument.

What Are the Preconditions of Intelligibility of the Argument?

Our final stop on the AIP checklist is the P—*preconditions of intelligibility*. This sounds more intimidating to some and sometimes people have a harder time grasping this one over the first two but don't give up! The "P" is a very powerful apologetic because it's like "pulling the rug out from underneath" the false view. It could also be likened to "holding up a mirror" so they can see that their worldview is nothing more than sinking sand. Dr. Jason Lisle, an astrophysicist and philosopher, calls it "nuclear strength" apologetics! Yes, it really is a powerful method of refuting false worldviews.

Preconditions of intelligibility really just asks, "What must be true prior to making this argument?" In other words, what must be predicated (what must be true) to make the argument in the first place? This can be done in many ways such as utilizing the foundational basis of:

- Laws of logic (rationality)
- Uniformity of nature (which make science and technology possible)
- Absolute morality (ethics)
- Reliability of senses (trusting our five senses: see, hear, smell, taste, touch)
- Reliability of memory (reliably remembering the past)
- Personal dignity and freedom (treating other people with respect)
- The existence of truth and knowledge
- Etc.

In a previous chapter I referenced "The Great Debate" between atheist Dr. Gordon Stein and Christian Dr. Greg Bahnsen. That debate was a prime example of using the "P" as Bahnsen used the laws of logic to totally undermine Stein's atheistic/materialistic position.

Given Stein's stated worldview, only material things can exist (like matter and energy), nothing *immaterial*—such as logic—can exist in his worldview (if he wants to be consistent). Since logic is not made of material, then logic doesn't exist, if Stein's position is correct. Since Stein admits logic does exist, his worldview is false. His professed worldview couldn't account for the very laws of logical debate that he was in! (At that point in the debate, Stein realized that "the rug had been pulled out" from underneath him!)

So when looking at the *preconditions of intelligibility*, simply ask the question: "What must be *predicated as true upfront* for something to make sense?" These are the *preconditions of intelligibility*. If the worldview being argued can't account for these preconditions—and yet it's assuming those are true—the worldview must be false.

Our example was from the atheistic worldview, which can't account for logic, the laws of nature, truth, or morality (none of those are material, after all), but other worldviews (e.g., Hinduism, New Age, paganism, Buddhism, etc.) also fail to account for these preconditions, which we will get into in subsequent chapters. In fact, you'll find out it's only the biblical worldview that can provide a basis for these preconditions of truth, knowledge, logic, morality, observable and repeatable science, and so on.

As you share the gospel with others, refuting their false worldview and pointing them to Christ, keep this "AIP checklist" in mind to help you do an internal critique of the unbeliever's arguments.

4 Abbreviated Logical Fallacies

"Come now, and let us reason together," Says the LORD, "Though your sins are like scarlet, They shall be as white as snow; Though they are red like crimson, They shall be as wool." (Isaiah 1:18)

"Mr. Ham, if God created us, who created God?" I was once asked this question by a 10-year-old boy—and I've also been asked it by middle-aged atheists. In response to the young boy I said, "Well, if someone made God then you would have to have a bigger God. But now, you have a problem, who made the bigger God? You would then need a bigger, bigger God who made the bigger God who made God."

I continued, "Now, you have a problem." Nodding, the boy said, "I know."

"Who made the bigger, bigger God? Now, you would need a bigger, bigger, bigger God who made the bigger, bigger God who made the bigger God who made God."

The boy understood my point—we could keep going back with bigger and bigger and bigger and bigger forever and then have to keep going.

The only thing that makes sense is that you would have to have the biggest God of all, the infinite, eternal God of the Bible. The only one true God who has always existed, who had no beginning.

I was using logic with this young boy to help him understand a foundational biblical principle and an attribute of God: our Creator is eternal and self-existent.

One way of using logic while discussing the Bible, and worldviews, is by learning to spot bad logic (when someone is being illogical). This sharpens your own thinking, trains you to make good arguments, and helps you dismantle the poor arguments that unbelievers often make. And, yes, people (believers and unbelievers) often make very poor arguments! But why are so many people illogical?

Of course, the primary answer is sin—we don't think properly because our minds are affected by sin. So the sad state of the culture when it comes to thinking shouldn't surprise us. Romans 1 describes what happens when God gives a nation over to be judged. It says they become, they became futile in their thinking:

> *For the wrath of God is revealed from heaven against all ungodliness and unrighteousness of men, who by their unrighteousness suppress the truth. For what can be known about God is plain to them, because God has shown it to them. For his invisible attributes, namely, his eternal power and divine nature, have been clearly perceived, ever since the creation of the world, in the things that have been made. So they are without excuse. For although they knew God, they did not honor him as God or give thanks to him,* ***but they became futile in their thinking****, and their foolish hearts were darkened. Claiming to be wise, they became fools.* (Romans 1:18–22; ESV, emphasis added)

Ever since sin entered the world (Genesis 3), sinners struggle to think properly. Consider the mind of unbelievers:

- Their mind is debased (Romans 1:28[1])

1. And even as they did not like to retain God in their knowledge, God gave them over to a debased mind, to do those things which are not fitting. (Romans 1:28)

- Their mind is blinded and veiled (2 Corinthians 3:14[2])
- Unbelievers have futile minds and their understanding darkened and blind (Ephesians 4:17–18[3])
- The mind is hostile to the things of God (Colossians 1:21[4])
- Sinful minds are carnal with false humility (Colossians 2:18[5])
- The unbeliever is depraved/corrupt in mind and truth (1 Timothy 6:3–5[6])
- Their mind is given over to Satan (2 Timothy 2:25–26[7])
- The unbelieving mind is corrupt (2 Timothy 3:8[8])
- Sinful minds are foolish, disobedient, deceived and lustful (Titus 3:3[9])

But, beyond sin and God handing a nation over to futility, a secondary reason so many people are illogical is that well, by and large, people today were never taught basic logic. They've merely been taught *what* to think, with no instruction on *how* to think (you need both!). And yet, understanding logic is foundational for proper logical and critical thinking and reasoning.

---

2. But their minds were blinded. For until this day the same veil remains unlifted in the reading of the Old Testament, because the veil is taken away in Christ. (2 Corinthians 3:14)
3. This I say, therefore, and testify in the Lord, that you should no longer walk as the rest of the Gentiles walk, in the futility of their mind, having their understanding darkened, being alienated from the life of God, because of the ignorance that is in them, because of the blindness of their heart. (Ephesians 4:17–18)
4. And you, who once were alienated and enemies in your mind by wicked works, yet now He has reconciled. (Colossians 1:21)
5. Let no one cheat you of your reward, taking delight in false humility and worship of angels, intruding into those things which he has not seen, vainly puffed up by his fleshly mind. (Colossians 2:18)
6. If anyone teaches otherwise and does not consent to wholesome words, even the words of our Lord Jesus Christ, and to the doctrine which accords with godliness, he is proud, knowing nothing, but is obsessed with disputes and arguments over words, from which come envy, strife, reviling, evil suspicions, useless wranglings of men of corrupt minds and destitute of the truth, who suppose that godliness is a means of gain. From such withdraw yourself. (1 Timothy 6:3–5)
7. In humility correcting those who are in opposition, if God perhaps will grant them repentance, so that they may know the truth, and that they may come to their senses and escape the snare of the devil, having been taken captive by him to do his will. (2 Timothy 2:25–26)
8. Now as Jannes and Jambres resisted Moses, so do these also resist the truth: men of corrupt minds, disapproved concerning the faith. (2 Timothy 3:8)
9. For we ourselves were also once foolish, disobedient, deceived, serving various lusts and pleasures, living in malice and envy, hateful and hating one another. (Titus 3:3)

What Is Logic?

Logic is defined by Merriam-Webster's Dictionary as,

> "*Logic*, used strictly in the singular, is a science that deals with the formal principles of reason."[10]

Simply put, logic is the study of correct and incorrect reasoning. It is a powerful tool but not a tool made of material things (like atoms). Rather, logic is an *immaterial* construct (you can't trip over logic!). Yet all of creation obeys logic, which gives us a taste of how God uphold His creation in a reasonable way (Hebrews 1:3[11]).

One of the most fundamental laws of logic (and one of the easiest to intuitively understand) is the ***Law of Non-Contradiction*** which states that something cannot be "A" and "Not A" in the *same relationship* and at the *same time*. In other words, you cannot have a drink in your hand and not have a drink in your hand at the same time and in the same relationship.[12]

A fallacy is when an argument violates sound logic or sound reasoning ("sound" meaning it's a valid argument, with true premises, and, thus, a true conclusion). Sometimes an argument can violate more than one fallacy at once. There are ***informal*** and ***formal*** fallacies. I'll give a listing of these in a moment.

The tool of logic becomes essential when dealing with ***arguments***. By argument, I don't mean a "yelling match" or a "comment war" but rather I use argument in the classical sense: an exchange/dialogue on differing views. An argument can consist of ***premises*** (certain accepted information), ***propositions*** (chain of statements and premises that are assigned a truth value [true or false]), and ***conclusions*** (using propositions and premises to lead to another truth claim). Arguments can be ***deductive*** or ***inductive***.[13]

---

10. Merriam-Webster Dictionary, https://www.merriam-webster.com/dictionary/logic, accessed July 29, 2020.
11. Who being the brightness of His glory and the express image of His person, and upholding all things by the word of His power, when He had by Himself purged our sins, sat down at the right hand of the Majesty on high. (Hebrews 1:3)
12. Other fundamental laws of logic include the "law of identity" [A is A] and the "law of excluded middle" [either A or non-A].
13. As a clarification, inductive and deductive reasoning are being used and defined as they relate to pure logic. This contrasts with inductive or deductive Bible study, which is defined differently. In in-depth Bible studies, inductive and deductive are methods of expounding on Scripture, whether topical or exegetical, and differ in the manner in which they arrive at conclusions. It is common for definitions to have crossover but be different in different fields of study (e.g., *entropy* in thermodynamics vs. *entropy* in genetics).

For **deductive** arguments, the conclusion is said to be *definitely true* if the premises are true (which, of course, is not always the case, but rather is usually "taken for granted"), and it is either *valid* if the conclusion follows from the premises, or it is *invalid* if the conclusion does *not* follow the premises.

Here's a simple example: (1) all marsupials give birth to underdeveloped young; (2) koalas give birth to underdeveloped young; (3) therefore, koalas are marsupials. In this argument, the conclusion (3) follows from the premises (1 & 2), so the argument is valid.

However, following our Aussie animal theme, here's an example of how an argument can draw a false conclusion from true premises: (1) nearly all marsupials are native to in Australia; (2) opossums are marsupials; (3) therefore, opossums are native to Australia. Even though the premises (1 & 2) are true, the conclusion (3) is false (opossums are the only marsupials that live in North America) and does not follow from the premises, thus a logical fallacy.

For **inductive** arguments, the conclusion is said to be *likely* or *probably* true, but not definitely true. The argument is considered strong if the conclusion is likely to be true given the premises. Otherwise, it is considered weak. A simple example would be: (1) Ken Ham dislikes chicken; (2) Emzara's Buffet at the Ark Encounter serves chicken; (3) therefore, Ken Ham doesn't eat at that restaurant. In this argument, the conclusion (3) is supported by the premises (1 & 2), so this is a reasonable, but not a particularly strong, argument.

However, additional information can change even a strong argument into a weak one. Using the above example: (1) Ken Ham dislikes chicken; (2) Emzara's Buffet at the Ark Encounter serves chicken; (3) Emzara's Buffet also serves a wide variety of delicious protein options; (4) therefore, Ken Ham doesn't eat at that restaurant. By adding another premise (3), the conclusion (4) is now no longer likely to be true, so this is a weak argument. (And, for the record, even though I don't like chicken, I eat at Emzara's—the buffet is delicious and many of our guests rave over the fried chicken!)

Lastly, there is also ***propaganda***, which usually involves some form of manipulation to influence public opinion. Propaganda isn't necessarily true through any logical means but the manipulation is often very effective. For example, advertisements will urge viewers to, "Buy this latest device before it's all sold out!" This is a type of propaganda (called "exigency") that uses language to manipulate you into quickly making a decision to buy a product.

Some of these terms may seem new, but, whether you realize it or not, you deal with logic all the time. These names (like premises, propositions, propaganda, and so on) are just the names we give to the various parts and types of an argument. You don't necessarily need to remember them, just keep the big picture in mind as we look at some of the most commonly used Informal Fallacies, Formal Fallacies, and Propaganda Types.

Common Informal Fallacies

> "So you don't care about women, and you just want them to die in back-alley abortion clinics because they can't get the reproductive care that they need?"

This is an example of a ***question begging epithet***. Rather than using sound logic to defend the pro-abortion (really, pro-murder) position, this person just throws out an emotionally loaded statement. The emotion, rather than the reasoning (which is very poor in this example), becomes the argument. This is a logical fallacy, but it can be quite convincing to many people because emotions are powerful. Watch out for emotive language designed to distract from the low-quality of the argument.

> "Elephant populations in Mozambique are evolving with half of female elephants no longer having tusks, due to pressure from poaching. This is a clear example of Darwinian evolution."

This is an example of an ***equivocation fallacy***. In this short paraphrase of a 2024 news article, the author describes an observable change within a population (natural selection)—elephants with tusks are poached, leaving only those who naturally do not have tusks (either due to mutation or genetic variation) to reproduce and therefore pass on tuskless genes to their descendants. The author calls this shift in the population "evolution" but then later uses the same word to refer to the unobserved idea of molecules-to-man (Darwinian) evolution.

But small changes within a population are not the same thing as molecules-to-man evolution, which requires the gain of new information and a change in kind, neither of which were observed (the elephants remained elephants). Evolution in the sense of "change" (natural selection) occurred, evolution in the sense of common descent did not.

When someone defines a word in an argument and then switches (equivocates on) the definition to apply what they've just demonstrated to an entirely different idea, they've committed an equivocation fallacy.

> "Either you accept and celebrate LGBTQ lifestyles, or you're a hateful bigot."

This is an example of an ***either-or fallacy*** (sometimes called bifurcation). In this example, you're given two options: celebrate these sinful choices, or be a hateful bigot. See the problem? There are more than two possible options!

As a Christian, I believe God's Word is truth, and God knows what is best, so I stand opposed to LGBTQ lifestyles out of love for lost people who need Jesus, not the temporary and deceitful satisfaction that sin brings (which ultimately, like all sin, leads to slavery and death).

When someone presents two (or more) options and acts as if other options don't exist, they've committed an either-or fallacy.

> "You're just a stupid idiot looking to make a buck off religious suckers."

I've been called worse—but this G-rated example will suffice for an ***ad hominem fallacy***. Rather than dialogue with the actual point you are making or present a logical counterargument, many times people will simply start slinging mud, stringing together obscenities, and insulting you. These arguments are directed against the person making the claim, rather than the claim itself. And that's not a good way to make an argument!

> "Genesis teaches living things don't change – that God created them how they are – and yet we observe creatures changing, therefore Genesis must be false."

This is an example of a ***strawman fallacy***. Here the evolutionist has completely misrepresented what Genesis says and then dismantled his false version of creation. Genesis teaches God created things according to their kinds, not their modern-day species. This allows for variation within a kind, but one kind won't change into another kind. In other words, creationists don't believe God created creatures exactly as they are today (for example, there weren't poodles in the Garden of Eden—just representatives of the dog kind).

Rather than deal with the text of Genesis, or the arguments creationists actually make, this evolutionist has "strawmanned" (misrepresented) the creation viewpoint and then attacked the false version he created. Of course, Christians can be guilty (often accidentally) of doing this too, that's why we should make sure we understand, as best we can, what our opponent *actually* believes, not what we think they believe.

> "The Bible can't be true because there's the parting of the Red Sea, floating axe heads, dead people coming back to life, and men surviving in a fiery furnace. Miracles violate the laws of nature."

In this example our opponent has just committed the ***fallacy of begging the question***. She has simply assumed what's she attempting to prove: the Bible contains miracles, miracles violate the laws of nature, therefore the Bible isn't true. Of course, miracles violate the laws of nature—that's what makes them miracles! The question is, can an all-powerful God who created the laws of nature not suspend or "violate" them to accomplish His divine purposes? If that's possible (and it is!), then there's no problem with miracles in the Bible.

Common Formal Fallacies

> "If the earth really is millions of years old, we should find fossils. Since we find fossils, the earth is millions of years old."

This argument is an example of the ***fallacy of affirming the consequent*** (these formal fallacies are usually written with a specific "if p, then q" notation, which you can see in the Formal Fallacies table on page 44). This is a fallacy because the premise affirms the consequent (the conclusion). You can see how arbitrary it is by simply substituting "the global flood" for "millions of years" and the argument still "works" because it hasn't really argued for anything!

> "If dinosaurs and humans lived at the same time, we'd find fossils of them together. We don't find humans and dinosaurs together in the same rock layers so they couldn't have lived at the same time."

This argument (similar to the one above) is an example of ***affirming the antecedent***. In this argument, the second premise denies the one that comes before (the antecedent). It's easy to see how fallacious this argument is—there are many reasons dinosaurs and humans wouldn't be buried together during a global flood. For one, they likely didn't live in the same area!

These formal fallacies are a little more difficult to wrap your head around, but they are common, so I encourage you to spend some time studying the formal notations in the Formal Fallacies table on page 44.

Common Propaganda Tactics

> "But what about the woman who was raped and is pregnant? Shouldn't she be able to get an abortion?"

This is an example of an (sadly very successful) ***appeal to pity***, a common propaganda type. Every person should feel immense pity for a woman who has suffered this kind of brutality and evil against her. But the pity and compassion we feel for the woman should not distract from the fact that the baby in her womb is a living human being, made in God's image, and, like the mother, a victim of the sin of an evil man. The man deserves to suffer for his sin; the innocent baby does not deserve the death penalty.

> "Every rational person believes in evolution."

This is a fallacy (***either-or fallacy***) but it's also a type of propaganda, specifically ***the bandwagon variety***. Basically, it's a way of saying "everybody's doing it!" But, as your mom may have said, if everyone is jumping off a bridge, would you do it? Or, think of it this way, everyone but eight people at the time of Noah were wrong about the coming global flood. Just because everyone else has jumped on the bandwagon, doesn't mean we should too!

> "Transwomen are women."

Not only is this an absurd argument because if men can be women than neither man nor woman means anything—but I digress. I'll use this as an example of the ***propaganda of repetition***. Sometimes all you need to do to convince someone of something is repeat it over…and over…and over again! Eventually a lie, or an absurd argument, repeated enough times "becomes truth" in the minds of many.

> "You fundamentalist Christians are just on the wrong side of history."

Who wants to be on the wrong side of history? Well, no one—and that's what makes the ***appeal to progression*** form of propaganda so convincing to many people. With this tactic, people are convinced that the way of progress, the way of the future, is whatever the person is advocating for and if they don't believe it (or buy it) they'll be left behind.

Conclusion

Logic is a powerful means of helping us take the "emotion" out of an argument and see the truth for what it is. And, actually, the existence of logic is powerful evidence for the existence of God. You see, logic is predicated on a logical God existing and upholding the world in a logical state. If the universe is just the result of random processes over millions of years, why should it behave in a logical, orderly way? Why would our brains work in a logical way? And where would an immaterial law of logic come from in a strictly material universe?

Logic stems from who God is. God knows all things and is never wrong on any matter and is the very standard for logic and truth. In fact, "God's logic is built into the universe, and that is why the universe consistently obeys natural laws and is not simply random or chaotic."[14]

As a side note, some critics claim that laws of logic are just arbitrary "inventions" made up by the Western world (does that make them racist? By today's woke definitions it probably does!). But it's easy to see that this claim is absurd. It's based on nothing more than arbitrary conjecture and, if it were true, then rational debate would be impossible since both sides could simply pick whatever standard of reasoning best suits them (i.e., both sides would be the "winner" according to their own arbitrary standard).

No, laws of logic are not subjective, man-made conventions, nor are they arbitrary laws that exist outside of God's being. These laws are rooted in God's own nature (God cannot contradict Himself, for instance), and, thus, are objective, universal, and unchanging.

We, as beings made in the image of a logical God, are able to understand and use logic in this sin-cursed world, where people are often illogical, to make sense of things. So learn proper logic and train yourself to do better at reasoning and not get caught up in "futile thinking."

---

14. Rob Webb, *"What Are the Laws of Thermodynamics, and How Do They Confirm Biblical Creation?"* Virginia Christian Alliance. https://vachristian.org/what-are-the-laws-of-thermodynamics-and-how-do-they-confirm-biblical-creation/

Listing of Some Informal Fallacies

- **Linguistic (Language) Fallacies**

1. **Emotive Language Fallacy** (Words lacking defined language – usually biased to upset someone) – *Question Begging Epithet; Epithet Fallacies*
2. **Ambiguity Fallacy** (Vague, general words)
3. **Equivocation Fallacy** (Using more than one sense of the word, tone, paraphrasing, multiple interpretations of a word, or incorrect assumption about a word) – *Bait-And-Switch Fallacy*
4. **Misinterpretation of a Statement Fallacy** (Not just a word – violations of context) – *Contextual Fallacy*
5. **Figure of Speech Fallacy** (Misusing idioms)
6. **Composition Fallacy** (Using a statement to judge the whole, using some small thing to illustrate the whole thing) – *Part-to-Whole*
7. **Fallacy of Division** (Dividing things that are not divisible or using the whole to judge one statement [opposite of Composition]) – *Whole-to-Part*
8. **Vicious Abstraction Fallacy** (Changing the argument to something else to try to prove the other point)
9. **Either-Or Fallacy** (Making someone choose between two things when there are other possible options) – *False Dilemma; Bifurcation; False Dichotomy; Trifurcation* (Like bifurcation but with limiting to three possibilities when more exist)
10. **Double Standard Fallacy** (Saying one thing and doing another or applying something unequally, depending on who is making the case) – *Special Pleading*
11. **No True Scotsman Fallacy** (Defining a word or argument in such a biased way to protect the argument from rebuttal)

- **Irrelevant Evidence Fallacies**

1. **Irrelevance Fallacy** (Introducing and/or jumping to disproving the wrong point) – *Red Herring; Irrelevant Thesis*

2. **Ignorance Fallacy** (Assuming something is true because one is ignorant to the subject)
3. **Pity Fallacy** (Pity or looking for sympathy)
4. **Respect Fallacy** (Giving airs to truth due to prestige, respect, etc.)
5. **Disrespect Fallacy** (Condemning an argument because of where/how/who began it) – *Genetic Fallacy*
6. **By Force Fallacy** (Making everyone think it is the truth by force and power)
7. **Attack the Person Fallacy** (Attacking the person, not the point) – *Ad Hominem*
8. **Prejudice/Masses Fallacy** (Appeal to the masses, prejudice of groups) – *Appeal to the People*
9. **Strawman Fallacy** (When someone attacks or refutes a distorted view of what their opponent believes instead of their actual position)
10. **Slippery Slope Fallacy** (Absurdly extrapolating)
11. **Guilt by Association Fallacy** (Falsely trying to link one group or set of ideas to another known group or known set of ideas that is false)

- **Material Fallacies**

1. **Fallacy of Accident** (Apply a general rule because of an obscure event)
2. **Converse Fallacy of Accident** (Come up with science rules and laws based on accidents)
3. **False Cause Fallacy** (Because something randomly happened by accident doesn't mean it always will or just because something happened before something else doesn't mean it caused the other) – *Post Hoc/Post Hoc, Ergo Propter Hoc*
4. **Failed Step Fallacy** (Conclusions do not follow the logic) – Non Sequitur
5. **Compound Questions Fallacy** (Using one or more questions to try to trick the opponent) – *Compound Question Fallacy; Loaded Question Fallacy, Complex Question Fallacy, Fallacy of the False Question, Fallacy of Many Questions, Trick Question Fallacy*

6. **Begging the Question Fallacy** (Using itself to prove itself in an arbitrary sense) – *Circular Reasoning, Petito Principii*
7. **Agreeable Fallacy** (Agree because you do it yourself) – *Tu Quoque*
8. **Misplaced Authority Fallacy** (Asking an expert to give an opinion about something he is not an expert in) – *Faulty Appeal to Authority/ False Authority Fallacy*
9. **Genetic Error Fallacy** (Determining if it is true by who is saying it now)
10. **False Analogy Fallacy** (Using a similar argument to argue the point regardless of different circumstances) – *Weak Analogy*
11. **Insufficient Evidence Fallacy** (Using inadequate evidence to jump to a conclusion) – *Lack of Evidence*
12. **Contrary to Fact Conditional Error Fallacy** (Alters historical facts and draws conclusions from them)
13. **Contrary to Premise Fallacy** (Self-contradicting right from the start)
14. **Hasty Generalizations** (Generalizing about a class or group based on a small sample)
15. **Reification Fallacy** (Treating abstract concepts, objects, and events of nature as real things with human characteristics) – *Anthropomorphic Fallacy; Anthropomorphism*
16. **Personification Fallacy** (A type of reification fallacy that treats animals as though they have human characteristics)
17. **Pathetic Fallacy** (A type of reification fallacy reflecting human feelings, actions, or emotions through inanimate objects)
18. **The Fallacy Fallacy** (Just because there is a fallacy doesn't mean the conclusion must be wrong – sometimes a conclusion can still be right even when falsely-argued)
19. **The Offense Fallacy** (Something is wrong merely because someone is offended by it)

Formal Fallacies

As noted, two common formal fallacies include *Affirming the Consequent* and *Denying the Antecedent*, both of which are *improper* forms of good logical flow called *Modus Ponens* and *Modus Tollens*.

Note: Unlike the informal logic that we just covered, which uses ordinary language, in formal deductive logic, it's common to use symbols such as **p** and **q** to represent any generic propositions in an argument (i.e., assessing the argument without knowing the actual meaning of the propositions). Also note that it's common to use short-hand notation, as shown below, when writing an argument (i.e., rather than writing "if p is true, then q is true," it's shorter to write "if p, then q").

(1) If p, then q. (2) p. (3) therefore, q.	Valid; *Modus Ponens*
(1) If p, then q. (2) q. (3) therefore, p.	Invalid; *Affirming the Consequent Fallacy*

(1) If p, then q. (2) Not q. (3) therefore, not p.	Valid; *Modus Tollens*
(1) If p, then q. (2) Not p. (3) therefore, not q.	Invalid; *Denying the Antecedent Fallacy*

An excellent example of an **Affirming the Consequent Fallacy** is:

If millions of years is true (p), then we should find fossils (q).
We find fossils (q), therefore millions of years is true (p).

This is one of the most common fallacies I've seen in a secular worldview, and it is espoused over and over again. This could just as easily be reversed for creation (just switch the words "millions of years" with "Creation and the Flood") which shows the arbitrariness of the fallacy.

Propaganda Types

Propaganda is very commonly (and successfully) used information to get people to act on or believe something often presented in a biased or misleading way. Advertisements are mastery at this:

- "Get it while it lasts, supplies are limited!" – *Exigency Propaganda*
- "Everyone else is doing it, come and join in" – *Bandwagon Propaganda*
- "Get the latest gadget" – *Appeal to Technology Propaganda*
- "Stop being old-fashioned and join our movement because we are progressive" –*Appeal to Progression Propaganda*

Specific propaganda types:

1. **Appeal to Fear** (Trying to get people to do something or else there may be consequences that you don't want to happen)
2. **Appeal to Pity** (Trying to get you to do something out of pity)
3. **Bandwagon** (Pressuring because many others are doing it)
4. **Exigency** (Giving time limits to influence you)
5. **Repetition** (Repeating something so many times that people begin to believe it regardless of the facts)
6. **Transfer** (Trying to transfer a thought of one thing/person to another thing/person)
7. **Snob Appeal** (Trying to get people to think they are better than everyone else)
8. **Appeal to Tradition** (Trying to influence due to tradition or age)
9. **Appeal to Technology** (Trying to influence via the latest thing)
10. **Appeal to Progression** (Trying to influence through the construct of progress)

Getting Started

Great is our Lord, and mighty in power; His understanding is infinite. (Psalm 147:5)

Where Do We Start?

For 50 years I've been teaching people to think foundationally. This means we start our thinking (we build our worldview) from the foundation of God and His Word. And that's the apologetics strategy of this book because "where do we start?" is really the crux of the debate about the existence of God and the truthfulness of His Word. We start with God because God starts with God!

Where Does *God* Start?

Yes, God starts with Himself—the ultimate authority in all matters. In other words, God doesn't start with man, nor does He start with logic or evidence from rock layers, fossils, planets, DNA, or any other created thing.

He starts with Himself. And this is clearly seen from the *very first verse* of Scripture, where God doesn't try to "argue" or "prove" His existence—He simply declares His existence as the supreme Creator of everything:

> *In the beginning God created the heavens and the earth.* (Genesis 1:1)

This is repeated in a similar way in the first verses of the Gospel of John:

> *In the beginning was the Word, and the Word was with God, and the Word was God. He was in the beginning with God. All things were made through Him, and without Him nothing was made that was made.* (John 1:1–3)

This makes sense; God is the self-existent and uncreated Creator who is omniscient, omnipotent, omnipresent, and eternal (He lives in *eternity* beyond time). God, being the ultimate and final authority on all matters *must* start with Himself—anything else makes no sense.

And God being the absolute authority is *consistent* throughout Scripture. Consider when God made a promise—who did He swear by and why?

> *For when God made a promise to Abraham, because He could swear by no one greater, He swore by Himself.* (Hebrews 6:13)

Where Should *We* Start Then?

So then, where do *we* start? The answer should be obvious: if God starts with God then so should we. And if we're starting with God that means we're starting with His authoritative revelation to us, the Bible, as well because it was written by God and therefore comes with the authority of God Himself (2 Timothy 3:16[1], 2 Peter 1:21[2]).

Starting with the God of the Bible—which is the way God does in His Word (e.g., "In the beginning God…")—automatically takes you in one direction and one direction alone: that God exists, and His Word is true. This critical point is *key* to our entire discussion: With God and His Word as our starting point, we have a *basis* for truth, logic, and knowledge

1. All Scripture [is] given by inspiration of God, and [is] profitable for doctrine, for reproof, for correction, for instruction in righteousness. (2 Timothy 3:16)
2. For prophecy never came by the will of man, but holy men of God spoke as they were moved by the Holy Spirit. (2 Peter 1:21)

to exist—and why we are made in such a way as to even recognize and understand logic, knowledge, and truth (and so much more).

You see, we're made in the image of a truthful, all-knowing, logical God (Genesis 1:26–27[3]). The Bible is the starting point for all *intelligibility* because God is intelligible and the absolute standard for intelligibility, thus giving us a rational basis for all *preconditions of intelligibility* (which we covered in previous chapters).

Again, don't get caught up with the big words—it simply means the Bible must be true for logic, knowledge, truth, and so on to exist. If you want another big word, the Bible must be *predicated* as true before we can even begin any argument or have any knowledge claim at all! (In fact, the ability to even speak coherent sentences would be impossible if the Bible was not true!)

For instance, when someone asks, "how do you know God exists?" they are assuming certain things just to ask the question. They are assuming *knowledge* exists. They are assuming *truth* exists. They are assuming that we are *made in such a way* as to understand logic and conclusions, questions and answers (i.e., being made in the image of an intellectual and communicative God), and assuming we know who God is (as defined in the Bible). So philosophically, we must ask, *what must be true* for this question to make sense? (i.e., How do we know *anything* is true?)

And that's where your starting point comes in. To be consistent, your starting point must be the authority of God and His Word. Without it the ability to reason and argue doesn't even make sense. As Dr. Greg Bahnsen once wrote about his mentor Dr. Cornelius Van Til:

> "Van Til urged Christians to be ever cognizant of the uniqueness of what God has revealed about Himself, developing their theology and apologetics with utter consistency and personal loyalty to His Word."[4]

---

3. Then God said, "Let Us make man in Our image, according to Our likeness; let them have dominion over the fish of the sea, over the birds of the air, and over the cattle, over all the earth and over every creeping thing that creeps on the earth." So God created man in His own image; in the image of God He created him; male and female He created them. (Genesis 1:26–27)
4. Greg Bahnsen, *Van Til's Apologetic: Readings & Analysis*, Presbyterian and Reformed Publishing, Phillipsburg, New Jersey, 1998, p. 275; as a point of note, Greg Bahnsen died in 1995 having finished the manuscript but the actual publication date was posthumous in 1998.

God started with God, so we should be loyal to God and start with God too. But from a big picture perspective, if you decide to start somewhere other than God, you're by default starting with a lesser authority like *man*. And starting with man is an active denial that God is an authority higher than oneself.

That is, when someone is starting with themselves, they intrinsically oppose starting with God. Philosophically, this is called "autonomous human reasoning," meaning human-based (which is necessarily fallible) reasoning *apart* from God. In other words, man is seen as the "supreme authority" over God at the very beginning of any argument.

And when it comes to your starting point there really are *only* two options: "God" and "not God," which, of course, is ultimately man. One is the supreme authority on all matters, and one isn't. So the real battle raging in the "does God exist?" question is really "who is your authority?" You only have two choices: God or man.

But the simple truth is that God is the absolute authority, and man isn't (again, God must exist or logic, morality, truth, etc. likewise don't exist because they have no foundation). When someone objects to God's absolute authority they've already committed a logical fallacy (faulty appeal to authority/false authority fallacy/misplaced authority fallacy).

Starting with arbitrary man's opinions in opposition to God and His authoritative Word, starts with a fallacy, destroys the only foundation for absolute logic and absolute truth (i.e., intelligibility), and takes you down a road where man is seen as a substitute or counterfeit authority in place of God.

It's the same poisonous lie from the garden, "You will be like God..." (Genesis 3:5). By substituting ourselves as the ultimate authority, we make ourselves our own *"god"* instead of submitting to the authority of the one true God. Obviously, these two different starting points build two very different worldviews. And both cannot be true at the same time—remember the Law of Non-Contradiction from the last chapter?

Furthermore, when people start with themselves as the authority, they are assuming certain things about themselves to be true. For instance, self-identity and logical thought about oneself have to come from some foundation—and the only position that makes ultimate sense is they stem from a logical God making us in His image, which allows thoughts about ourselves to even be possible. And the person must also assume that they exist (*identity* in logic) and that they are made in such a way as to think logically about themselves—and that only makes sense if they're made in the image of a logical God (and not in the image of a rock, for instance).

So even though people may claim to start with themselves (thus, fallaciously having no basis for identity and logic), they really aren't starting with themselves but rather *borrowing* aspects of a biblical worldview (probably unbeknownst to them!) while actively attempting to usurp God's authority.

To truly start with man, then the *preconditions of intelligibility* must also be given up—which leaves that person without a logical basis for anything at all and a list of logical fallacies they've already committed.

So, where do we start? *The God of the Bible is where we start.* There is no other logical option! Without God and His Word, there is no basis for logic, truth, knowledge, and so much more. We must, just to recognize our own existence, start with God's revealed Word. To give up God and appeal to yourself as the "supreme authority" is to commit "intellectual destruction" right from the start.

Popular Apologetics Methodologies – And Their Problems

Every Christian should be an apologist.

Now that doesn't mean every Christian will have immediate answers to every objection or should get up on a stage and debate an atheist. It just means we should be prepared with answers whenever we are called on to defend the hope we have in Christ. As discussed in the last chapter, we do this by standing on the authority of God's Word, starting with God first. This is the only proper basis from which to start our apologetic.

There are a variety of apologetic methodologies used throughout history, and even today, to defend the Christian faith. But is every method equal? In other words, does every method follow the biblical pattern of starting with God and His Word as the ultimate and absolute authority? You see, the Bible isn't silent on this issue of apologetics but tells us how God wants us to respond and defend the faith, for instance:

- *We destroy arguments and every lofty opinion raised against the knowledge of God, and take every thought captive to obey Christ, being ready to punish every disobedience, when your obedience is complete.* (2 Corinthians 10:5–6; ESV)

- *Preach the word; be ready in season and out of season; reprove, rebuke, and exhort, with complete patience and teaching.* (2 Timothy 4:2; ESV)
- *"...but in your hearts honor Christ the Lord as holy, always being prepared to make a defense to anyone who asks you for a reason for the hope that is in you; yet do it with gentleness and respect."* (1 Peter 3:15; ESV)

Don't Give Up the Bible!

"Don't answer me with the Bible—I don't believe it!"

Many Christian apologists foolishly fall prey to the idea that because the person they are speaking to doesn't believe the Bible, they must leave the Bible out of the debate and make their case strictly on "human terms." They think this will somehow make their argument more convincing.

But think about it: If you give up the Bible at the very beginning of the debate, why even bother doing apologetics (which is commanded in the Bible) in the first place? See the tension? Yet far too many Christians have done exactly this!

Scripture is the ultimate authority in all areas, and so our defense is to affirm that authority in our "argument" or response. If the Scriptures really are the ultimate authority, it would be illogical (and sinful!) to toss the Bible aside and argue as if there is *some other* "absolute authority." If you do that, you've lost the debate before it even began!

As we discussed in the last chapter, if you don't start with God, then by default, you start with man and "autonomous human reasoning" (reasoning *apart* from God and His Word). You're making fallible man the absolute authority, not God. And, whether you realize it or not, that is the foundation of the religion of humanism. Why would a Christian argue for the Christian religion assuming the religion of humanism is true? It's an irrational approach to defending the Christian faith! Yet, sadly, it's very common.

The goal of the Christian apologist is to *always* be honorable to God's Word (i.e., as stated in 1 Peter 3:15, "in your hearts honor Christ the Lord as holy…") and refute false claims about God and His Word while preaching the good news of Jesus Christ—His death, burial, and Resurrection. The gospel message of Christ taking our punishment for us on the cross really is good news because it's the only way sinners can be saved from the infinite wrath of God, who should rightly punish us for our sins because He is a righteous judge. Everyone needs to hear and believe this message! That's why we do apologetics.

In defending God's Word and the gospel, we must *never* give up *any* of the 66 books of the Bible (it's God's Word—not our clever arguments, after all—that changes people's hearts). Rather, by using the Bible and standing firmly on Scripture, we're to effectively "silence" the opponent's arguments. Dr. Cornelius Van Til once wrote:

> "This view of Scripture, therefore, involves the idea that there is nothing in this universe on which human beings can have full and true information unless they take the Bible into account."[1]

Don't be like so many Christians who abandon the very Word they're supposed to be defending! And that means you have to be careful in your apologetics methodology.

Three Apologetic Methods

While others exist, the three most common apologetic methodologies that Christians tend to use are *classical* apologetics, *evidential* apologetics, and *presuppositional* apologetics. The classical and evidential methodologies are similar because they both have the same starting points, same processes, and considerable overlap but they do have *different focuses*, as you'll see below.

The presuppositional apologetics approach (also called the *transcendental* method) has a different starting point, a different method, and an overall commitment to an ultimate authority.

So which apologetic method is the best to use, or can they all just be tools in a toolbox to be used depending on the situation?

To answer that, we need to (1) understand each of these methods and then (2) test them against the absolute authority of God's Word. This may surprise you, but, yes, *even the apologetic methods* used to defend God's Word need to be humbly tested against God's Word (e.g., 1 Thessalonians 5:21[2]). So let's do that, starting with an introductory overview:

---

1. Cornelius Van Til, *Christian Apologetics*, Presbyterian & Reformed Publishing, Phillipsburg, New Jersey, 1976, 2003, p. 20.
2. Test all things; hold fast what is good. (1 Thessalonians 5:21)

1. **Classical:** This philosophical method attempts to demonstrate the existence of God starting with "natural theology" (e.g. cosmological, teleological, moral arguments) and then moves into using evidence (e.g. reliability of the biblical text, resurrection of Jesus, etc.) to argue that the Christian God is the God who you've just demonstrated exists.

   This method assumes and begins with autonomous rational thought (man's reasoning) as the "absolute standard" regarding philosophical debates. Evidence is often used in conjunction with the argument, but it's important to understand all evidence is *interpreted based on a given worldview*. Popular Classical apologists include men like William Lane Craig, Thomas Aquinas, Norman Geisler, R.C. Sproul, and J. P. Moreland.

2. **Evidential:** As the name suggests, this method begins with the evidence (e.g. manuscript evidence, archaeological evidence, Old Testament prophecy, etc.) and argues that Christianity is the best explanation of the available evidence.

   Like classical, this method also starts with autonomous rational thought as the "absolute standard." It assumes that when people evaluate the evidence, they might come to the right conclusion regarding Christianity in general. In other words, the apologist starts with human logic to look at the evidence and then tries to point to the Bible's truthfulness. This method assumes people are "neutral" in their judgments about God and His Word and that people just need "more evidence" to be convinced of the truth of God's Word. Popular evidential apologists include B.B. Warfield, William Paley, and John Warwick Montgomery.

3. **Presuppositional**: This method assumes at the beginning of the argument that Christianity is true. In this method, God and His Word are the absolute and only standards of morality, logic, uniformity in nature, science, etc. In other words, the Bible provides the only basis for a worldview that makes knowledge possible. All other worldviews must borrow from the Bible to even try to make sense of the world.

This method is sometimes called "Van Tillian" (named after Cornelius Van Til who articulated it in modern times). Along with Van Til, other popular presuppositional apologists include Greg Bahnsen, Kenneth Gentry, Michael Butler, John Frame, Jason Lisle, James White, and Jeff Durbin, along with historical apologists such as Augustine (in some aspects) and John of Damascus.

Other popular semi-presuppositional methods include:

- **Clarkian**: This method leans heavily on logic and the Bible as the only source of truth. According to its "founder," Gordon Clark, the best worldview is the most logical, and Christianity is the most consistent in its logic. So Christianity appears to be the best.
- **Schaefferian**: Francis Schaeffer used his variant of presuppositional apologetics to push other worldviews to their logic conclusions, highlighting their inconsistencies and ultimate despair. He argued the best worldview will give the best answers to life. Since Christianity gives the best answers to life, Christianity is the correct worldview.
- **Carnellian**: Edward J. Carnell argued that the best worldview is the most coherent and produces moral transformation (is ethically verified). Christianity is the most coherent and produces that moral fruit, therefore Christianity is the right worldview.

A few other less popular methods will be briefly discussed in the next chapter.

Who's Your Authority?

A key difference between these apologetic methods is their ultimate starting point: God's Word (presuppositional apologetics) vs. man's word (classical and evidential apologetics). In this book I'll argue for presuppositional apologetics because, as I've stated previously, Christians shouldn't start with fallible human reasoning—we must start with God's Word, as God Himself does.

> *Trust in the LORD with all your heart, And lean not on your own understanding; In all your ways acknowledge Him, And He shall direct your paths. Do not be wise in your own eyes; Fear the LORD and depart from evil.* (Proverbs 3:5–7)

When Christian apologists start anywhere *other than God* and His Word, they are giving up God and His Word as the supreme authority in their argument. In other words, if you give up God's Word, you forfeit the very thing you set out to prove before you even began!

Imagine you're a soldier and, while charging into battle, your opponent yells: "Before we begin, you must drop your sword, and be *neutral* in this fight!" If you agreed, you'd lose your weapon—but he still holds his! That would be incredibly foolish and you would immediately lose the fight. Yet that's what Christians do when they start with man's word, leaving the Bible out of the discussion. They've thrown down their sword. But the Bible makes it clear there's no neutrality.

> *He who is not with Me is against Me, and he who does not gather with Me scatters abroad.* (Matthew 12:30)

> *Because the carnal mind is enmity against God; for it is not subject to the law of God, nor indeed can be.* (Romans 8:7)

> *Adulterers and adulteresses! Do you not know that friendship with the world is enmity with God? Whoever therefore wants to be a friend of the world makes himself an enemy of God.* (James 4:4)

By abandoning your sword, you aren't neutral. You've simply changed from the foundation that God's Word is the authority to man's word.

Now imagine you're a soldier in that same battle but, rather than using your sword to strike down your opponent, you begin by first trying to convince the other soldier that your sword is actually a *real* weapon. And so, you start describing everything about it, from its metal composition, to how it was made, to where it came from, to how long it is, how sharp it is, and so on. Again, this would be foolish! And yet so many Christians today do that with their apologetic! There are times where you will use evidence to point to the truth of Scripture, but if you're a Christian, stop spending all your time defending your sword by trying to "prove" its existence—*just use it!* (Ephesians 6:17[3], Hebrews 4:12[4]).

Here's the bottom line: Any defense of Scripture *must* be predicated on the Bible; that is, it ought to *presuppose* (and, thus, be foundationally presuppositional) that Scripture is the authority—not man's word.[5] When we

3. And take the helmet of salvation, and the sword of the Spirit, which is the word of God. (Ephesians 6:17)
4. For the word of God is living and powerful, and sharper than any two-edged sword, piercing even to the division of soul and spirit, and of joints and marrow, and is a discerner of the thoughts and intents of the heart. (Hebrews 4:12)
5. Though some would argue this is fallacious circular reasoning, this article explains why it is not: "Circular Reasoning." https://answersingenesis.org/logic/the-fallacy-of-begging-the-question/

start with the Bible, we are thinking God's thoughts after Him and emulating Him, which is what every Christian is commanded to do! The way He looks at things is the correct way, and we should mimic this.

A Closer Look: Classical, Evidential, and Presuppositional Apologetics

Classical and Evidential

Classical and *evidential* apologetics have a long history, going back to the days of classic Greek philosophy and men like Socrates, Plato, and Aristotle (these pagan men lived as the Old Testament era was ending). With Greek philosophy human logic is considered supreme.

Christian apologists, using these methods, start from that same foundation with human logic serving as the ultimate authority for building arguments. With such a similarity, how can you tell the difference between them? Well, if the arguments are based strictly on reason and philosophy, then it is *classical apologetics*; if the arguments are dealing with historical or scientific "facts" and evidence, then it is called *evidential apologetics*. Of course, there's overlap—every apologetic method (except *Fideism*) eventually uses evidence.

As we've already discussed, human logic is not a bad thing—logic is *essential* in any form of debate and is only possible because the Bible is true when it says we are made in the image of a logical God of truth who upholds everything in a consistent, logical way. Hence, when starting with the Bible, we have a true, justified belief for the existence of logic. But if you start with man you automatically *reject* God's Word as the ultimate starting point...so why should logic *exist*? Why would a Christian have an apologetic method that starts like that?

Consider the power of starting presuppositionally, even when it comes to logic—you can use the existence of logic to defeat nearly every other religious tradition. For example:

- In any materialistic worldview (where matter/energy is all that exists), logic cannot exist because it is not made of matter/energy. This is the most common worldview among secular scientists—those who use logic/reason daily when doing science for a living!

- In any Eastern religion (like Hinduism, Taoism, etc.) where "all is spirit" and "all is one" (monism), then being logical and being illogical are essentially one and the same (whether they realize it or not); hence, logic shouldn't exist given that worldview.
- In any pagan, moralistic, or mythical religion where "man is the best there is" (such as in Buddhism, Confucianism, paganism, Greek Mythology, Wicca/Witchcraft, etc.), logic is purely human dependent. Thus, logic becomes arbitrary and fallible because humans are arbitrary and can err, which means logic is ultimately meaningless in any of these religions.

Of course, those who don't start with God's Word generally agree that logic does exist, yet their worldview can't account for it, so how do they get around this? They *borrow* or, more accurately, *steal* the basis and existence of logic from God whether they acknowledge it or not.

But many Christians don't start this way. They've fallen into the trap of using classical or evidential methods, basically setting aside the Bible as the absolute authority to then attempt to argue a logical case using philosophy or evidence grounded in human reasoning. This means they're really just arguing for some sort of a *generic god's* existence (not the God of the Bible). Or perhaps, in some cases, the truthfulness of one verse or phrase in the Bible.

Imagine a "stepping stone" to go from "a god exists" to the leap that it's the God of the Bible that exists or that the Bible is trustworthy (e.g., at least one passage or this one part of the Bible is *likely* truth, so *maybe* all of it is too). This is called an *inductive* argument (as opposed to a *deductive* argument, as we discussed in previous chapters), where the claim isn't necessarily shown as true but could be probable or likely.

With these methods, once you've convinced your opponent that the Bible *might* be true on some of its claims or that a god *might* exist (or at least a "good probability" of it), then you can "kind of" use the Bible after that. Of course, apologists for Mormonism, Islam, Hinduism, Greek mythologies, etc., can do the same thing—use human reasoning and generic arguments for a god to then leap to their particular god or gods and their "holy" books or myths. Many different religions can and do use this methodology (that should be a red flag right there for Christians!).

Presuppositional Apologetics

Presuppositional apologetics starts with God and His Word as the foundational starting point.

This apologetic method essentially looks at philosophy, world religions, reason, facts, and evidence the same way every time—in light of God's Word as the absolute authority. It starts from the foundational presuppositions that:

- man is fallible and therefore not in a position to usurp God the Creator's authority,
- that facts and evidence don't "speak for themselves" or that they are somehow "neutral" – they are always interpreted,
- that God's Word is our starting point to correctly interpret evidence and facts to confirm Scripture. In other words, we do not use facts/evidence to "prove" God's Word is true. Our powerful Creator has spoken and revealed Himself to us, and that's why we know His Word is true.

As I've said before, when people reject God's Word as the authority when looking at any kind of evidence, facts, or philosophy, they, by default, place man in the position of ultimate authority—and that's not neutral! When someone claims to be "neutral," he's already said the Bible is wrong and, thus, is not actually being neutral.

At the foundation, Van Tillian presuppositional apologetics places God and His Word, the Bible, as the absolute authority in every area. God, who knows all things and cannot lie, has stated in the Bible that all other worldviews are wrong. By extension, all other worldviews have inconsistencies—and must borrow from the Bible to make any sense of the world at all—whether they realize it or not. The other worldviews just do so inconsistently.

Christianity alone is consistent and provides the only basis for the *preconditions of intelligibility* (preconditions to make knowledge possible). All other worldviews are arbitrary, inconsistent, and lack the preconditions that make knowledge possible (recall the "AIP" test from the previous chapter). So, presuppositional apologists not only point out where false worldviews contradict God's Word, but they also do an internal critique of the unbelievers' worldview to show where it is arbitrary, inconsistent, and where they lack the preconditions necessary for knowledge within their own worldview. It's both defensive and offensive.

Consider presuppositional apologetics vs. atheism, a popular religion in our Western world:

When the Creation Museum opened in May 2007, a group of atheists protested the opening, including by hiring a small airplane to fly above the museum pulling a banner that read, "Thou shalt not lie."

Now, in their own worldview atheists have no reason not to lie—they have no ultimate foundation for morality—so to accuse us of lying by teaching the Bible as real history, they had to borrow from the Christian worldview.

The only reason right and wrong exist is because we have an absolute authority, the God of the Bible, who defines and sets the standard for what is right and wrong in the Bible. These atheists didn't have a foundation to determine right and wrong—only their subjective opinion! In fact, given their worldview, for an atheist to say something is "right" or "wrong" ("good" or "evil") is really no different than saying "I don't like relish on my hot dog"—it's just a personal preference. Oh, and to wrap up the airplane story, our guests kept telling me they thought we'd hired the plane to tell the world to stop lying! It really didn't go the way the atheists thought it would.

Or here's another one. Atheists believe that we are just animals and yet most are wearing clothes. Do animals wear clothes? No. So instead of making a consistent argument that we are only animals, atheists are instead *confirming* (whether they realize or not) a literal Genesis 3 where we wear clothes due to sin and shame (Genesis 3:21[6])!

This works with many other everyday things: Why do we have a 7-day week? The Bible. Why does logic/reason exist? The Bible. Why does knowledge exist? The Bible. Why is marriage defined as a man and a woman? The Bible. This list goes on. But in an unbeliever's worldview (not just atheism), they lack the very foundational basis for such things.

But Watch Out!

What I've laid out above is called the Van Tillian method,[7] named after the man who systematically laid it out. Others have contributed some

6. Also for Adam and his wife the LORD God made tunics of skin, and clothed them. (Genesis 3:21)
7. Please note this is not an apologetic for everything Van Til said. He had specific denominational views that, as a non-denominational ministry, we do not take a stance on.

excellent material to expand on his work, but beware that these other presuppositional views have some overarching flaws that reduce the potency of their overall thrust because they drift from God's Word as the standard. As Bahnsen points out[8] regarding the three most popular semi-presuppositional views:

Clarkian: Gordon Clark essentially says that the best worldview is the most logical, and Christianity is the most consistent in its logic. So, Christianity appears to be the best. His overall viewpoint falls short of being presuppositional because he argued that man's autonomous reasoning (man apart from God) should be used as the "absolute" starting point in one particular instance: logic. This conflict led Clark to argue that "logic was God" to get around the inconsistency.[9] This is a clear problem that plagues his methodology.

Schaefferian: Francis Schaeffer essentially says that the best worldview will give the best answers to life. Christianity gives the best answers to life. So, Christianity appears to be the best. Schaeffer's apologetic ultimately ends up appealing to man's authority over God's Word, placing humans as the "authority" to judge what are the best answers for life.

Carnellian: Edward J. Carnell essentially says that the best worldview is the most coherent. Christianity is the most coherent via the internal text. So, Christianity appears to be the best. This method also moves from God's Word to autonomous human reason in certain areas, specifically coherency.

While each of these men did some great apologetic work, here is the problem that each of these "presuppositional" methods have in common: by what standard? Is it "best" to start with autonomous human reason or God's Word? By moving away from God's Word as the absolute standard in certain areas, these other methods really move away from a true presuppositional apologetic. They fail because they still need to stand on the *preconditions of intelligibility* in regard to the Bible's absolute standard just to *make* their case.

---

8. To understand these viewpoints and their overarching flaws please consult *Presuppositional Apologetics: Stated and Defended* by Dr. Greg Bahnsen, edited by Joel McDurmon, American Vision (and Covenant Media Press), Powder Springs, GA, 2008.
9. Greg Bahnsen, *Presuppositional Apologetics: Stated and Defended*, edited by Joel McDurmon, American Vision Press, Powder Springs, Georgia, 2008, pp. 137-196. See also Gordon Clark, *The Johannine Logos: The Mind of Christ*, Presbyterian and Reformed Publishing Company, Phillipsburg, New Jersey, 1972 to see how he tried to justify it by the grammar of John 1:1.

Each of these other views are only partially presuppositional because they all ultimately rely on fallible human logic as the absolute standard in some area, instead of God, who is the ultimate standard in all areas. Did you notice that in each of these views some form of human logic is elevated above God? In a true presuppositional apologetic, logic is a tool, but it is still subservient to God and His Word—the ultimate authority—since logic is only possible because God and the Bible are true.

Another problem with each of these views is they *can't* really allow you to know the Bible is 100% true, or to be 100% certain that God even exists, or to be 100% certain of one's own salvation. Their position really is that Christianity is the "best possible worldview right now," "likely the most coherent so far," and "gives the best possible answers right now"—but could still be wrong. (Notice the lack of firm, faithful commitment to God's authority in each of these statements!)

Essentially, each of these other alleged "presuppositional" views are forced into a position that biblical matters are likely "true" or likely the "best" possible option—but we can never *know* it with complete confidence. Interestingly, the Bible says we *can know* numerous things. For example:

- And we **know** that all things work together for good to those who love God, to those who are the called according to His purpose (Romans 8:28).
- But whoever keeps His word, truly the love of God is perfected in him. By this we **know** that we are in Him (1 John 2:5).
- These things I have written to you who believe in the name of the Son of God, that you may **know** that you have eternal life, and that you may continue to believe in the name of the Son of God (1 John 5:13).

See It In Practice: Classical Apologetics

Got Questions defines classical apologetics this way:

> Classical apologetics is a method of apologetics that begins by first employing various theistic arguments to establish the existence of God. Classical apologists will often utilize various forms of the cosmological, teleological (Design), ontological, and moral arguments to prove God's existence. Once God's

> existence has been established, the classical apologist will then move on to present evidence from fulfilled prophecy, the historical reliability of Scripture, and the bodily resurrection of Jesus to distinguish Christianity from all other competing forms of theism.[10]

In classical apologetics, the starting point is logic as the apologist attempts to build a coherent case of a generic "theistic being." Again, this is a *Greek* method, used by ancient Greeks like Aristotle, to argue for the existence of *a god*.

Classical apologetics is a two-step method: first argue for the existence of a *god(s), supreme being, absolute reality*, or a *universal principle* that might exist beyond nature—that is, make a case for generic "theism." Then move into showing Christianity and the biblical God as the God you've just "proved."

The primary four classical arguments, often called "proofs" for the existence of God (even though they start with human reasoning, not an ultimate standard of God's Word, and therefore don't "prove" anything, but merely make a probable case), are:

1	*Cosmological Argument*
2	*Teleological Argument*
3	*Ontological Argument*
4	*Moral Argument*

These arguments are used as the first step in moving the unbeliever toward Christianity. So how good are these arguments for the existence of a god? (Spoiler alert: They're not good!)

Cosmological Argument

The cosmological argument assumes that a human understanding of logic is absolute, and then builds the argument specifically on the fundamental logical law of *cause and effect*. Here's how it goes: every effect has a cause (i.e., everything that had a beginning must have had a series or "chain" of causes) and if you go back far enough, there is a *first* cause or *initial* cause

10. "What is classical apologetics?," Got Questions, accessed 3/31/2023, https://www.gotquestions.org/classical-apologetics.html.

that is then defined as "deity," "initial force," Brahman, nothing (e.g., big bang), or God/a god, depending on the apologist's worldview.

There are problems with this argument:

1	It assumes the law of cause and effect, which exists in the observed universe (and is assumed to work in the whole universe), also works outside of time and prior to the existence of the universe and space-time. But we were not there to observe that, so this is an unprovable assumption.
2	It assumes this "theistic being" upholds logic and the universe consistently, at all times and in all places. But without knowing the character of this being, how can we know this? How do we really know the law of cause and effect hasn't changed in the past? How do we really know this law works everywhere in the world? Or how do we really know this law will work the same tomorrow as it does today? We can't know any of this unless an all-knowing God, who is outside of space-time, has revealed that to us! The God of the Bible promised to uphold the world in a particular way (e.g., Genesis 8:22, etc.) so we can know the laws of logic and the laws of the universe have been held up in a certain unchanging way (except for the case of God's miraculous working if He chooses to do so), and He promises to continue to uphold the universe in the future. But the Bible isn't part of the discussion at this point in the cosmological argument, which means one can't really know if the law of cause and effect goes prior to the universe or even back into the past since the Bible's been left out of it!
3	The unknown "god" in this view is also being subjected to the laws of the universe but is not necessarily above and beyond them. Hence, this "god" may not be all-powerful – just "powerful enough" to get things started. Furthermore, this initial cause doesn't necessarily have to have a mind but can be an impersonal force like the universe creating itself as in the big bang or an Eastern religion (e.g., impersonal Brahman's manifestation of Brahma of Hinduism). In other words, you're far from proving the God of the Bible!

This argument can be used to argue for a big bang just as much
as a creator. You see, in the secular view, the naturalistic big bang
would be that first cause. Sadly, many Christians today use this
naturalistic story as an apologetic tool, saying "God used the big
4 bang as the first cause to create the universe." Not only does this
contradict the clear teaching of Scripture, and attempt to add
man's ideas into Scripture, but it really means God didn't do anything since the big bang is a model that says the universe created
itself with no God required.

Having a first cause isn't necessarily an exclusive argument for the God of the Bible—which even most atheists recognize! It would be *consistent* with the God of the Bible, but it isn't necessarily a case for the God of the Bible only.

Teleological Argument

The teleological, or design, argument looks at design in nature and then attributes that design to a designer(s) (e.g., intelligent design arguments). If we find design in the universe (e.g. fine-tuning of the solar system for life) or nature (e.g. DNA), there must be a designer.

Again, this only gets you so far because who is that designer? People from various religions have used this argument to argue for their alleged god(s). In fact, atheists even use this argument to argue for extraterrestrial aliens or some sort of "higher intelligent" life that exists somewhere out in the cosmos that maybe even seeded life on earth millions of years ago. So, this is *not* an argument exclusively for the God of the Bible.

Now this doesn't mean design in nature is never a good argument. When we start with the Bible (like Romans 1:20[11]) we expect to find design as God is the ultimate designer and engineer. In other words, design is a confirmation of Scripture and the history God gives us in Genesis. When we start with Scripture, we know that people have no excuse for denying God's existence because it's obvious from what He's made that He exists (Romans 1:18–21[12]). But we use design to confirm the truth of the Bible, not as the starting point for our arguments.

11. For since the creation of the world His invisible attributes are clearly seen, being understood by the things that are made, even His eternal power and Godhead, so that they are without excuse. (Romans 1:20)

12. For the wrath of God is revealed from heaven against all ungodliness and unrighteousness of men, who suppress the truth in unrighteousness, because what may be known of God is manifest in them, for God has shown it to them. For since the creation of the world His invisible attributes are clearly seen, being understood by the things that are made, even His eternal power and Godhead, so that they are without excuse, because, although they knew God, they did not glorify Him as God, nor were thankful, but became futile in their thoughts, and their foolish hearts were darkened. (Romans 1:18–21)

Another major problem with starting with design is that this is a fallen world! Nature is filled with beauty, yes, but also so much ugliness and even supposed "bad design." Atheists are often quick to point out that nature seems designed "red in tooth and claw" with death, disease, and bloodshed everywhere. Without God's Word, and the history of a perfect creation marred by sin, as the starting point, a Christian can't answer this objection and ends up with a God who is not all-good or all-powerful but who made an imperfect creation—and that's certainly not the God of the Bible!

Of course, this supposed counter-argument is predicated on the existence of good and bad (which are biblical concepts) and that man is made in such a way as to study the world and have the ability to make conclusions about his observations (a biblical concept too!).

Unless the Bible is true, the teleological argument doesn't make sense at all. But if we start our thinking, and our apologetic, from the Bible, we can know with *certainty* that God's original creation was perfect, but now the world suffers under the curse of sin (Genesis 1:31,[13] Deuteronomy 32:4[14]), which explains why we see both "good" and "bad" design.[15]

Ontological Argument

The ontological argument starts with human reason alone (rather than the observation of evidence). The most common forms of this argument date back a thousand years to Anselm of Canterbury (a Christian philosopher and theologian of the eleventh century). He defined God as a being *which no greater can be conceived*, and being *the greatest*, must exist as that is the best thing since it is better than not *existing*. Another way to put it: Since God is the "greatest thing" possible, and since existing is better than not existing, God must exist.

If this argument seems a little convoluted, it is—and that's not the only problem with it!

13. Then God saw everything that He had made, and indeed it was very good. So the evening and the morning were the sixth day. (Genesis 1:31)
14. He is the Rock, His work is perfect; For all His ways are justice, A God of truth and without injustice; Righteous and upright is He. (Deuteronomy 32:4)
15. While "bad design" is sometimes a result of the effects of the curse, more often it only appears that way because scientists haven't figured out or do not yet understand the intended purpose for that thing (e.g., vestigial organs).

- Consider the ambiguity of the terms "great" and "exist" – what do they actually mean, without an ultimate standard to define them (remember, we can't use the Bible yet, only human reasoning).
- If the concept of God is just based on our reasoning, then different people can arbitrarily conceive different beliefs of who is the greatest "god" (Zeus, Allah, Brahman, God of the Bible, etc.).
- The concepts of good, great, greater, better, spiritual being, etc. ultimately only make sense if the Bible is true. So just to develop this argument, you have to assume the Bible's truth. But this defeats the purpose of an autonomous argument that tries to be distinct from the Bible!
- Christians want to define the greatest being as the "God of the Bible." But to do that, they have to give up the ontological argument and make a huge leap from "greatest being I can imagine" to the God of the Bible without "proving" the God of the Bible via the ontological argument – yes, that makes the argument as pointless as it sounds! The logic doesn't follow – which is ironic since the whole argument relies on pure logic.

Of course, I agree there is no one greater than the God of the Bible, but I only know that because He revealed it in His Word. But again, the Bible is not part of the discussion, and that really is the fatal flaw of this argument.

Moral Argument

The moral argument is based on the idea that all people have some sort of conscience or "moral code." Every person naturally knows that some things in our world are "right" (good) and some things are "wrong" (evil). Therefore, the argument goes, there must be some sort of (transcendent) moral lawgiver.[16] Though not everyone agrees on the exact same code, in many instances, people believe that "man is basically good," and so there must be an ultimate perfect lawgiver. But why assume this alleged deity is ultimate or perfect? That doesn't logically follow.

16. As a tie back to our previous chapter on logic, be aware Christian apologists will (sometimes unknowingly) present this argument in a way that commits a formal fallacy called *Affirming the Consequent*. (As a reminder, this fallacy takes the form of: (1) if p, then q. (2) q. (3) Therefore, p.) For instance, the argument is sometimes presented in this form: (1) if a moral lawgiver exists, then people have a moral code. (2) People have a moral code. (3) Therefore, a moral lawgiver exists. Again, it's important we point out fallacies in the unbeliever's arguments, but we also must be careful not to make the same mistake ourselves!

And, you may've noticed, there's a lot of *immorality* in the world! Does that mean there exists an ultimate immoral deity? That would be the religion of dualism (two distinct equal and opposite, good and evil, beings or gods). Or is there a lawgiver who is equally good and equally evil? (And who ultimately defines good and evil anyway?) In other words, just looking at the world around us won't get you to the God of the Bible!

This is similar to the arguments that Plato used with ideals and perfect forms that existed elsewhere.[17] One of his students, Aristotle, eventually called out Plato's error because there was no way to show *how* that ideal realm interacted with the real world. Now, a Christian could argue that the God of the Bible can impose His moral will on His creation (and that's true), but this means you've given up the argument and appealed to the Bible *without the argument yielding any proof* for the God of the Bible! In other words, it's pointless. Just start with the Bible in the first place!

If you merely assume there's a perfect standard of morality, and that our human morality reflects a broken aspect of that morality, the moral argument ultimately fails. Why assume that a perfect standard exists instead of assuming a broken moral standard form of "god" exists? And since man's morals are not absolute and not unchanging, why assume the nature of this god is absolute and unchanging? This is ultimately why the ancient Greeks arrived at the conclusion that their gods' morality was not absolute but had a changing nature (i.e., their gods were more like super-humans with fallible natures).

Again, there's a huge leap to get from the moral code most humans sort of hold to, to the unchanging, perfect, absolute God of the Bible—and to make that leap, you have to use the Bible!

Oh, and when it comes to the standard of morality, who picks it? Who says? Without the Bible, sinful man does. The only way to know that absolute morality exists *is by revelation* from an absolutely moral God. So, the moral argument doesn't lead to an absolute God, but an absolute God does lead to absolute morality. Therefore, the argument is actually reversed (back to front). When one starts with God and His revealed Word, we have a basis for absolute morality.

---

17. Plato, *The Republic*, in Classics of Western Philosophy, edited by Steven M. Cahn, Hackett Publishing Company, 1977, 3rd Edition, Indianapolis, Indiana, pp. 112–190.

Just Start with the Bible!

Many Christians use these arguments because they sincerely want to point people to the God of Scripture (that's a good thing!). But each of these classical arguments for the existence of "a god" always require a gigantic leap to say the god is the *God of the Bible.*

Furthermore, each of these four arguments for the existence of the absolute, all-knowing (omniscient), all-powerful (omnipotent), present everywhere (omnipresent), perfectly truthful God of the Bible started by assuming that God's absolute authority doesn't apply in philosophy—that's a big problem! It's putting ourselves as the authority over God.

Instead of starting with our own wisdom, have faith in God and the power of His Word (Hebrews 4:12[18], 11:6[19]) and don't lean on your own understanding (Proverbs 3:5[20]). Look at everything the way God does (by using His Word as a lens/worldview), and so think God's thoughts after Him (Proverbs 1:7[21]). Only then can we begin to make sense of good and bad, design, first cause, logic and reasoning, morality, and so on. All of these things are a *confirmation* of what we expect because God's Word is true:

- Is the God of the Bible the first cause? Yes, but we already knew that because of Genesis 1. The law of cause and effect exists because the God of the Bible upholds the world in such a way.
- Do we expect to find design? Yes. When we do, it's a confirmation of the Bible. Even when we find broken design, the Bible makes sense of that too (the fall) – hence, that is also a confirmation of the Bible.
- God is the absolute and the greatest being – and we can know that with certainty because He revealed it to us.

18. For the word of God is living and powerful, and sharper than any two-edged sword, piercing even to the division of soul and spirit, and of joints and marrow, and is a discerner of the thoughts and intents of the heart. (Hebrews 4:12)
19. But without faith it is impossible to please Him, for he who comes to God must believe that He is, and that He is a rewarder of those who diligently seek Him. (Hebrews 11:6)
20. Trust in the LORD with all your heart, And lean not on your own understanding. (Proverbs 3:5)
21. The fear of the LORD is the beginning of knowledge, But fools despise wisdom and instruction. (Proverbs 1:7)

- Absolute morality exists but only comes out of a biblical worldview where God is the absolute moral Lawgiver (being a reflection of His perfectly moral nature). Morals are meaningless without God giving them meaning and cannot even be defined without God defining them! Seeing morality (even broken morality in a broken world) is a confirmation of the truthfulness of Scripture.

Each of these arguments confirms the Bible—but only when we start with the Bible!

See It In Practice: Evidential Apologetics

While classical apologetics has been popular throughout church history, evidential apologetics is now far more popular due to the explosion of scientific advancements over the last few hundred years. But the core—human reason is the ultimate authority—of the two methods are really the same so you're about to see many of the same problems!

As I mentioned earlier, the difference between the two is in the specific focus: classical apologetics focuses heavily on philosophy and reason, evidential apologetics focuses heavily on *evidence*—like scientific observations or historical documents. And when it comes to the evidence, this method assumes our reasoning and interpretation is the ultimate starting point because "the facts speak for themselves."

Consider what one of the world's leading evidentialist apologists, John Warwick Montgomery, has said:

- "Facts must carry their own interpretations."[22]
- "The very nature of legal argument (judgments rendered on the basis of factual verdicts) rests on the ability of facts to speak for themselves."[23]
- "Evidential apologists of all stripes hold in common a second crucial aspect: the conclusions of the apologetic arguments they employ are **shown to be probable rather than certain**"[24] (emphasis added).

22. "Evidentialist Apologetics: Faith Founded on Fact," http://bible.org/seriespage/evidentialist-apologetics-faith-founded-fact
23. Montgomery, "*The Jury Returns: A Juridicial Defense of Christianity,*" in *Evidence for Faith*, 335.
24. "Evidentialist Apologetics: Faith Founded on Fact," http://bible.org/seriespage/evidentialist-apologetics-faith-founded-fact.

- "Can one 'begin with God' (the Christian God) without benefit of objectively discoverable historical facts? I say No."[25]

Did you notice that, like the classical method, the evidential method only tries to demonstrate that Christianity *might* be true? Thus, the method only provides *probabilistic* results (i.e., the Bible *might* be true on a particular point here or there). So, this method cannot lead to any absolute certainty about anything at all—its best arguments are only *probable*.

Evidentialism is largely inductive, as opposed to deductive, in its logical format (as discussed in previous chapters), rendering its arguments probable but not absolute. The format further evaluates "facts" based on human logic and opinions to make a probable case for Christianity on a specific point (such as the Resurrection, existence of Daniel, existence of Pontius Pilate, reliability of the Scriptures, etc.).

Right away there are some big problems:

- This falsely assumes unbelievers can interpret facts "correctly" when presented with them. In other words, it's believed that data and evidence don't need interpretation – they speak for themselves – but scientific data, historical documents, archeological finds, or any other piece of evidence *do* require interpretation! After all, none of us was there! And that interpretation is largely based on your already preconceived worldview.

  For instance, this is why creationists and evolutionists have the same evidence (e.g. rock layers), but don't agree on the interpretation (e.g. rapid deposition by a global flood vs. slow and steady deposition over long periods of time). Different worldviews lead to different interpretations about the past.

25. J.W. Montgomery, *The Philosophy of Gordon H. Clark: A Festschrift,* edited by Ronald Nash, Presbyterian and Reformed Publishing Company, Philadelphia, Pennsylvania, 1968, p. 383.

- Evidentialists interpret things based on man's opinions, attempting to judge God and His infallible Word by fallible human opinions. Yes, God, who is the judge of all matters and who judges by His Word, is being judged by fallible, sinful beings! This is back to front!

  No, God is the Creator and man is the creature, and it's nothing less than arrogant foolishness to think we can judge God. The Apostle Paul in Romans 9:20 (see also Isaiah 2:22[26]) put it this way: *But indeed, O man, who are you to reply against God? Will the thing formed say to him who formed it, "Why have you made me like this?"* Even though evidential apologists have the best intentions, their foundation is faulty!

Let's circle back to the big problem I mentioned earlier: these arguments are merely *probabilistic*, not certain or absolute. So the evidentialist cannot be *certain* that the resurrection really happened, or that the Scriptures are 100% reliable, and so on. Thus, they leave open the possibility that the resurrection *did not occur* or that the Bible is not 100% reliable.

This is a critical point because the bedrock of Christianity is at stake here: The evidentialist *cannot have absolute certainty* regarding anything written in Scripture—including the Resurrection, which is the foundation of the gospel itself (1 Corinthians 15). Furthermore, these arguments, if successful, can only say one small part of the Bible "might be true" (e.g., the Resurrection or certain prophecies) but not the whole of Scripture. And no matter your "high levels of confidence" or how much you think your explanation is the "best explanation," probability means there's always a chance the Bible's not true—and sinners will go with that slim chance!

So, to be consistent with his methodology, if an evidentialist is asked if he's saved, he should respond with, "probably" and when he gathers with the church on Sunday he's merely worshipping a God who probably exists—but I doubt that's how such a person thinks! And why not? Because they *know* they are saved and God exists—because the Scriptures say they can *know* (with 100% certainty!). But by their method, how do they really know that the Bible is 100% true, and thus that they are truly saved? Simply put, they can't, given their methodology. Note the inconsistency!

It's a leap of blind faith to go from the Bible being *"probably true"* to being *"100% true."* And yet, this is exactly what many evidentialists do in practice. They use a method to say the Bible "might be true" but then say they

26. Stop regarding man in whose nostrils is breath, for of what account is he? (Isaiah 2:22; ESV)

personally believe it to be 100% true. What just happened? Without any logical reason whatsoever, the evidentialist gave up his evidentialism (and its probabilism) to stand on the Bible as true!

Let me give you an example of this "probably true" line of reasoning. Richard Swinburne, a professor of philosophy at Oxford University, calculated in the early 2000s that the probability of Jesus' Resurrection was about 97%.[27] Others have also done this calculation and, based on their personal study (e.g., Dr. Gary Habermas), have come to numbers either higher or lower than Swinburne's result. But in each case, they leave open the possibility that the Bible is *not true* regarding the Resurrection!

But here's the irony: many evidentialists will cite Scripture as *true* to make an evidential case for the *truthfulness* of one of the Bible's claims. For example, how do they argue for the Resurrection being (probably) true? Typically, he or she will quote from the Gospels, Matthew, Mark, Luke, and/or John, *as truth* to understand specific circumstances surrounding the Resurrection (such as timings, witnesses, etc.) and then go on to make a probabilistic case for the Resurrection while trying to counter the critics.

Some evidentialists will go so far as to say that even unbelievers "agree" these passages are true, but now truth is dependent on unbelievers' opinions! No, the Bible is the truth in all matters and *not* dependent on the fallible opinions of unbelievers who are in hostile rebellion against their Creator.

But notice that by appealing to Scripture, the rug was just pulled out from underneath the evidential method because appealing to Scripture defeats the *very purpose* of the approach! Turning to the Gospel accounts as though they were trustworthy and true, without first attempting to show that these verses are trustworthy, just exposed the method's inadequacies.

This is the same category of error we saw with the classical approach—why not just start with the Bible first? If you have to give up your method in order to appeal to the Bible as the absolute truth…to then argue for the evidential method…well, you have a problem! What is the point of appealing to the evidential method if the Bible is already treated as the absolute authority, when the goal of the evidential method is to argue for the possibility of the Bible being the absolute authority?

In the evidential method, you can't know for certain that the quoted passages are even 100% true—the best you can get is *a good probability* of it.

27. Emily Eakin, "So God's Really in the Details?," *The New York Times*, May 11, 2022, https://www.nytimes.com/2002/05/11/arts/so-god-s-really-in-the-details.html.

So, with this method, when you get down to the "nuts and bolts," the Bible is rendered useless in the debate.

So why do Christians use this method? Well, some evidentialists argue that this approach mimics how the legal system in the modern West looks at the evidence. But our modern legal system is based entirely on human opinions being seen as the absolute truth—not God's Word. In fact, the Bible was tossed out of the legal system generations ago (and look at the mess we're in!). And actually this idea doesn't work for the evidentialist's presupposition that the facts "speak for themselves" because, even in the court room, evidence is interpreted in the light of man's preconceived ideas, opinions, and worldview. This is why the same piece of evidence can sometimes be used by both the defense and the prosecutor!

While those who use an evidential approach have good intentions (and most sincerely do believe the Bible!), and God can and does use our fallible human attempts to share the gospel to save, Christians should avoid this method of argumentation because it places man, not God, as the authority. Really, when interpreting the evidence, this method comes down to one person's opinion vs. another person's! But in reality it's always man's word vs. God's Word.

Rather than thinking that starting with the Bible "isn't the most effective" evangelism strategy, we should honor God and do apologetics the way He does it in Scripture—by starting with Him.

See It In Practice: Presuppositional Apologetics

Now let's look at apologetics from the proper starting point: God and His Word! Presuppositional apologetics starts with God and His Word as the absolute authority *on all matters*—including reason, logic, philosophy, scientific evidence, historical documents, archaeological finds, and so on, because it's in Christ that all the treasures of wisdom and knowledge are hidden (Proverbs 1:7[28]; Colossians 2:3[29]).

With this method we start with the presupposition that there is no greater authority than God—not human logic, our own reasoning, or the evidence. As the late Dr. Greg Bahnsen put it: "If God is God, then who or

28. Ibid. Ref. 21.
29. *In whom are hidden all the treasures of wisdom and knowledge.* (Colossians 2:3)

what authority could be higher than His? There cannot be an authority higher than God's."[30]

If one of the reasons for apologetics is to argue for God's Word being the absolute authority, then why give up the Bible as the absolute authority like the classical and evidential methods do? Rather, we start how God does—with God and His Word as the authority from the first verse of the Bible: "In the beginning God..." (Genesis 1:1).

Note that God didn't stop part of the way through Genesis 1:1 to suddenly use a classical argument for His possible existence, or an evidential method to present all the scientific evidence to say His statement "might be true." No, He just says it!

In other words, the Bible comes with God's own *self-attesting* authority. And rightly so! God is the final authority, and only He can reveal Himself by final authority. God treats Himself as the ultimate authority, and that is why presuppositionalists also mimic what God does by using God and His Word as the ultimate authority.

The presuppositionalist recognizes that God and His Word are the ultimate presupposition—hence the name "presuppositional"(though, philosophically, this methodology is often known as "transcendental" apologetics). And here's what makes it so unique: Unlike classical or evidential methods, unbelievers, no matter their religion, *cannot* use this methodology. If they did, they'd have to give up their own worldview to do so! When we start with the Bible, the Word of God is not "off limits" at the beginning argument. In other words, you don't have to throw down your sword to start debating someone! Rather, you've *presupposed* the authority, sufficiency, and truthfulness of your sword, God's Word, right from the start.

But what if the unbeliever says, "Well, I don't believe the Bible"? Simply ask him, "By what authority do you object to God's absolute authority?" You see, he has committed the fallacy of *faulty appeal to authority* (a false authority fallacy/misplaced authority fallacy). Yes, he is being illogical when trying to oppose God's Word.

You see, the unbeliever already knows God exists. The Bible clearly says every person knows—not just that some general "god/deity" exists—but that they *know* in their heart of hearts that the God of the Bible exists (e.g., Romans 1:20–32) but they actively suppress this knowledge. And as

30. Dr. Greg Bahnsen, *Against All Opposition: Defending the Christian Worldview*, Powder Springs, Georgia, American Vision, 1998.

a result, as Romans 1 says, God has given them over to a debased mind to do what ought not to be done.

Because of this innate knowledge, the goal is *not* to convince them God exists. *They already know God exists*, but they suppress it through self-deception as they pretend He doesn't exist (e.g., atheism/agnosticism), by reinterpreting God (e.g., Hinduism, Islam, Jehovah's Witnesses), or convoluting Him to be one of many "gods" (e.g., Greek Mythology, Mormonism). One of the main goals of presuppositional apologetics, therefore, is to expose the *internal inconsistency* of the unbeliever's worldview, where they are being arbitrary, and where they are unknowingly borrowing from God's Word (e.g., wearing clothes, 7-day week, using logic, absolute morality, observable and repeatable science is possible, etc.)—and then we point them to Jesus Christ!

Remember that convincing someone of the arbitrariness or inconsistencies of their worldview, *does not save anyone* from the wrath of God over their sin. Remember that it is God who saves people—not us or our apologetic—but we present the gospel which is the power of God unto salvation (Romans 1:16) in the same way we do our apologetic—always using the Bible and the gospel as the ultimate authority. In other words, if we're not pointing people to the Cross, then we've ultimately failed in our apologetic.

In the same way that Jesus asked for the stone to be rolled away from Lazarus' grave, so we remove "stones" and stumbling blocks, but only God can bring people back to life. So we pray and we trust Him. And also remember that apologetics will not remove what keeps so many people from Christ: *pride*. Only the gospel can do that! (And be careful that apologetics doesn't "puff" you up with pride!) This is why the apologist's job is to humbly and respectfully "close the mouth" of the unbeliever and let the Holy Spirit convict the heart unto salvation (e.g., 1 Corinthians 12:3[31]).

So is presuppositional apologetics always just pointing out the problems with other worldviews and then turning to the gospel? No—we often use evidence to defend the truth of Scripture and answer skeptical questions. In a later chapter, I'll discuss the four proper uses of evidence in the presuppositional method but the short answer is: we present evidence *interpreted* in light of God's Word (remember, everyone interprets evidence within their own presupposed worldview).

31. Therefore I make known to you that no one speaking by the Spirit of God calls Jesus accursed, and no one can say that Jesus is Lord except by the Holy Spirit. (1 Corinthians 12:3)

When people misinterpret evidence for their respective religion, we correct their (mis)understanding of the evidence. Using a presuppositional approach, you might ask what must be true for this to be possible. Here's an example, you're asked, "How do you know the Bible is true?" Ask, "What must be true for someone to ask this question?" Or more simply, "How do we know anything is true?" The typical responses you'll hear from people are, "I know things are true based on reason" (i.e., it has to be rational) or "I know things are true based on observation" (i.e., using our five senses), or maybe, "I know things are true based on experience" (i.e., it just works for me).

Pause for a moment and ask yourself the same question, "How do we know anything is true?" Did you realize that to even ask the question, "How do you know the Bible is true?" (or any question at all!) you have to assume the Bible is true? Follow me for a moment.

- First, the question assumes absolute truth exists.
- Second, the question assumes knowledge exists.
- Third, the question assumes that human beings are made in such a way that we can use logic and reasoning to even understand the question itself.
- All those things are only possible...if the Bible is true! So just to ask the question means the Bible has to be true.

Now, this doesn't mean the unbeliever has to "believe" the Bible is true (I can guarantee that he won't!) but that the Bible must be true to even make sense of his questions in the first place.[32] Another way to put it: The Bible has to be true because of the impossibility of the contrary. That is, if the Bible isn't true, then we couldn't know anything at all. In fact, apart from the Bible, you wouldn't even be able to *make sense* of reality, and, thus, would be reduced to absurdity.

And we find many *confirmations* that the Bible is true in all different areas of science, archaeology, philosophy, and so on. But instead of any of these being the *basis* from which we argue for the Bible, the Bible is the absolute—and these things are merely *consistent with what we expect to find*—because Scripture is true.

32. Someone might argue that before the Bible was fully written you couldn't make this case, but that is also without warrant. God's Word existed prior to creation and just because it wasn't entirely revealed to man at different stages in history doesn't means it wasn't true from the moment God created time.

Did you notice how the Bible is used as the authority, not man's opinions or fallible human reason? And did you notice that any argument, evidence, philosophy, and so on are merely predicated on the truthfulness of God and His Word? This is what makes a presuppositional apologetic completely different from the classical and evidential approach.

Cornelius Van Til summarized it well when he said,

> "The best, the only, the absolutely certain proof of the truth of Christianity is that unless its truth be presupposed there is no proof of anything. Christianity is proved as being the very foundation of the idea of proof itself."[33]

So, the presuppositionalist acknowledges that logic, knowledge, truth, uniformity of nature, and absolute morality exists, and that these things are solely predicated on God and His revelation to man. Simply put, how we know things are true is because God has spoken.

But what about other religions—can no one else account for these things? Actually, no, they can't! For example:

- Atheists, if they were consistent, would have no laws (moral, logical, or scientific) since they are not material, and atheism is a materialistic religion (i.e., the only things that supposedly exist in atheism are matter and energy in the cosmos). In fact, given the atheistic worldview, whether something is "true" is actually meaningless! It's impossible to get truth from a brain that's just chemicals so the atheist cannot even trust that his own thoughts are telling him the truth. And, in his worldview, an atheist believes his worldview is "true," not because he freely chose to believe it's true, but rather as a byproduct of chemical reactions!

- Hindus believe all is "one" (called "monism") and, therefore, being moral and being immoral is "one and the same." It also means being logical and illogical are "one and the same." In other words, per their worldview, logic and reasoning mean nothing.

- Muslims (Islam) openly borrow from the Bible as the absolute standard for these things (e.g., Surah 2:40–42,126,136,285; 3:3,71,93; 4:47,136; 5:47–51, 69,71–72; 6:91; 10:37,94; 21:7; 29:45,46; 35:31; 46:11).

Like Islam, every man-made religion borrows from the biblical worldview in order to have any level of rationality, whether they realize it or

33. Cornelius Van Til, *The Defense of the Faith*, edited by K. Scott Oliphint, P&R Publishing, Phillipsburg, New Jersey, 4th Edition, 2008 (originally 1955) p. 381.

not. Muslims, as well as other cults of Christianity, often acknowledge it at least. (Actually, according to Islamic doctrine, their god, *Allah,* is said to be so "superior" that nothing in our human experience can even begin to compare. However, laws of logic are an essential *part* of our human experience, which means laws of logic cannot be a reflection of the way Allah thinks—and thus Islam cannot provide a basis for any kind of rationality, which is why Muslims have to borrow from the Bible to make sense of anything).

The presuppositionalist shows unbelievers that their worldview is wrong at its very base, as they can't make sense of logic, knowledge, truth, and so on. Then we teach them the correct worldview from God's Word, pointing them to Christ.

Paul did this in Athens, Greece when he was witnessing in Acts 17. He showed the Greeks that their worldviews were wrong and that God was the only one responsible for life, breath, and all things (Acts 17:25[34]), which includes logic, truth, knowledge, and so on. In short, the Greeks' false worldviews had no basis. Then Paul explained more about who God was, concluding with Jesus and the Resurrection. But notice from the text that Paul never asked them to judge God's Word to see what their fallible opinions led them to—but instead used God's Word as the authority to *judge their false beliefs* and thus call them to repentance.

The presuppositional approach gets to the root of the worldview issue, while still allowing the use of evidence and reason within biblical parameters. We let God be God, and His Word be the authority in all areas, including in our apologetic methodology.

Be Unashamed

While many apologetic methods have been used by Christians through the ages, they often abandon God's Word as the starting point. Therefore, all of those methods fall short. I encourage you as a Christian to unashamedly stand on the authority of the Bible in all areas, and thus stand presuppositionally on Scripture.

Use the Bible to judge all scientific evidence, historical data, philosophy, and archaeological finds against the Scriptures, and see how they are confirmations of His Word. Refute and demolish arguments and every

34. Nor is He worshiped with men's hands, as though He needed anything, since He gives to all life, breath, and all things. (Acts 17:25)

pretension that sets itself up against the knowledge of God and take captive every thought to make it obedient to Christ (Acts 18:28[35]; 2 Corinthians 10:4–5[36]). Do this with gentleness and respect (1 Peter 3:15[37]), and also with boldness, in obedience to our love for Christ (e.g., Acts 9:29[38]; 2 Corinthians 5:12–15[39]), with the ultimate goal of unashamedly proclaiming the Gospel.

---

35. For he vigorously refuted the Jews publicly, showing from the Scriptures that Jesus is the Christ.(Acts 18:28)
36. For the weapons of our warfare are not carnal but mighty in God for pulling down strongholds, casting down arguments and every high thing that exalts itself against the knowledge of God, bringing every thought into captivity to the obedience of Christ. (2 Corinthians 10:4–5)
37. But in your hearts honor Christ the Lord as holy, always being prepared to make a defense to anyone who asks you for a reason for the hope that is in you; yet do it with gentleness and respect. (1 Peter 3:15)
38. And he spoke boldly in the name of the Lord Jesus and disputed against the Hellenists, but they attempted to kill him. (Acts 9:29)
39. For we do not commend ourselves again to you, but give you opportunity to boast on our behalf, that you may have an answer for those who boast in appearance and not in heart. For if we are beside ourselves, it is for God; or if we are of sound mind, it is for you. For the love of Christ compels us, because we judge thus: that if One died for all, then all died; and He died for all, that those who live should live no longer for themselves, but for Him who died for them and rose again. (2 Corinthians 5:12–15)

Other Apologetic Methods That "Fare No Better"

But wait—there's more!

Besides classical, evidential, and presuppositional, there are yet more apologetic methods used for the existence of God. These methods are not nearly as popular, but you may encounter them from time to time so we'll briefly discuss them here, including:

- Fideism,
- "The Sheep Hear His Voice" method,
- Reformed Epistemology,
- and Cumulative Case.

Fideism

"I just have faith."

That statement summarizes our next apologetic approach: fideism. Fideism comes from the Latin word for "faith" and means "by faith alone."

In its most basic form, fideism means you don't defend the Christian faith or waste time giving an answer to the existence of God or the truth of the Bible. These truths are merely taken on faith alone (i.e., "just because").

There are quite a few people who hold to this view (I often encounter them in the comments section on my social media posts where I'm defending the faith!), but fideists often can't tell you they are fideists. Why? Well, many simply default to this position because they haven't taken the time to even understand the position or just apologetics in general.

Now, this kind of faith may at first seem commendable—they just believe based on faith and the Bible says it's impossible to please God without faith (Hebrews 11:6). But really it's a type of "blind faith" that's unlike biblical faith, which is a logical, defensible faith as mentioned in Scripture (e.g. Hebrews 11:1, "Now faith is the substance of things hoped for, the evidence of things not seen"). Biblical faith isn't unreasonable or arbitrary.

If the fideist is ever asked, "*How do you know God exists?*" the answer is usually something along the lines of, "I believe in God based on my faith" (notice the circular reasoning; "I believe because I believe"). They're not really answering the question and are ignoring the biblical commands to have answers for our hope (e.g. 1 Peter 3:15[1] and 2 Corinthians 10:4–5[2]).

It's easy to see the problems with this "method" by applying it in another context. A Mormon or a Muslim could just as easily defend their false gods by this same blind faith method of merely saying *they have faith in their gods. We've gotten nowhere!*

Fideism is an arbitrary "cop out" of an answer that doesn't really answer the question. Essentially, whether they realize it or not, fideists have an arbitrary *blind faith* when it comes to the existence of God instead of a logical, defensible faith.

1. But in your hearts honor Christ the Lord as holy, always being prepared to make a defense to anyone who asks you for a reason for the hope that is in you; yet do it with gentleness and respect. (1 Peter 3:15; ESV)
2. For the weapons of our warfare are not carnal but mighty in God for pulling down strongholds, casting down arguments and every high thing that exalts itself against the knowledge of God, bringing every thought into captivity to the obedience of Christ. (2 Corinthians 10:4–5)

The *Sheep Hear His Voice* Method

"I just know in my heart God exists."

According to this view, which isn't really a defined apologetic but one we'll nickname the "sheep hear His voice" method, the existence of God is known to us because of John 10:27, "My sheep hear my voice, and I know them, and they follow me" (ESV). In other words, you can know God exists and the Bible is His Word because we are Christ's "sheep" and follow Christ (the Shepherd), who is God. (This is a very feelings-based approach).

Notice that this entire method is predicated on the Bible being true in this passage—which adherents of this position have *not* shown. They are arbitrarily assuming the Bible is true *on this one point* to argue the Bible is true (so we can hear His voice) and, therefore, to say we can know God exists. It's merely assuming the very thing it is trying to prove but in an arbitrary (vicious circular) fashion.

And, when it comes to biblical interpretation and application, context is important. And the context of this passage has little to do with God's existence, but was a discussion Jesus had with some of the Jews, regarding whether or not He is the Christ (the Messiah they were waiting for) and God in the flesh. His miraculous works alone, done in God the Father's name, should have been enough for them to know that He is the Christ, but they didn't listen to Him.

In contrast, Jesus said that the "sheep" who hear His voice are those who know Jesus is *the Christ and follow Him.* As a result of this discussion, many of the Jews of His day wanted to kill Jesus for the crime of blasphemy. Within context, this passage is not a polemic on the existence of God—it's a discussion about whether Jesus is God, not whether God exists (the Jews He was speaking with already believed in God the Father).

Other passages used to support this method are 1 John 4:6–73 and Hebrews 11:6[4] and the idea that Christians know God exists because they "know in their hearts" by the power of the Holy Spirit. But here we have the same problem with applying these passages this way as with John 10:27: these passages are *disconnected* from the Word of God to act independently.

3. We are of God. He who knows God hears us; he who is not of God does not hear us. By this we know the spirit of truth and the spirit of error. Beloved, let us love one another, for love is of God; and everyone who loves is born of God and knows God. (1 John 4:6-7)
4. But without faith it is impossible to please Him, for he who comes to God must believe that He is, and that He is a rewarder of those who diligently seek Him. (Hebrews 11:6)

Therefore we no longer have the whole of Scripture to attest to the defining nature of who the Triune God is.

Again, this method arbitrarily picks and chooses certain verses to be true to then argue that the whole Bible is true concerning God and His existence. (This is also a logical fallacy called the *Fallacy of Composition*, where it's argued that what is true of the parts must also be true of the whole. It's like saying, "This one sentence in an atheist's book is true, therefore the whole book, including atheism, is true!")

This method is not technically starting with Scripture because it starts by subtracting a whole lot of Scripture and relying on human thoughts and feelings attached to a few disconnected passages. If the method would start with the whole of Scripture, then God would indeed exist without any need for this argument.

And think about it, if our own thoughts and feelings about God are our primary apologetic, what god are we really referring to? If you argue that you're talking about the *God of the Bible*, then you're not starting with your feelings, but appealing to the presuppositional approach of *starting with Scripture* to define who God is. Thus, the method fails—just start with all of Scripture.

And to this point, this is why if you've ever witnessed to a Mormon (Latter-Day Saint), you may've heard a similar kind of argument. In a nutshell, their argument for the existence of their gods (which is not the God of the Bible) is that they feel a "burning in the bosom" or "knowing in their heart" that causes a feeling of "security and truth" for them.[5]

In other words, they claim to know that their gods and the "inspired" writings from Joseph Smith (like the Book of Mormon) are really true because of an "overwhelming feeling" that it is right. So, if both the Christian and the Mormon are using the same argument of "knowing in their heart" that different God(s) exists, then who's right? One would still need an *objective* standard! Otherwise, the debate is just one subjective opinion/feeling against another. Thus, this method fails miserably.

5. In fact, this mantra is even posted on their LDS website.

Reformed Epistemology

> "I don't need proof to know God is real – belief in Him is properly basic."

This method (also known as foundationalism) was popularized in the 1980s by Alvin Plantinga with contributions by William Alston and Nicholas Wolterstorff. They recognized that the classical and evidential arguments for the existence of God fall short. However, this method still differs from presuppositional apologetics in various ways.

Reformed[6] epistemology (the philosophical term for the study of how we know things) was largely developed by Plantinga through responses to evidential objections. In his book *Warranted Christian Belief*, Plantinga outlines his methodology,[7] which is derived from what he calls the "Aquinas/Calvin model" (A/C model), named for Thomas Aquinas and John Calvin. He further developed that A/C model so his is often called the extended A/C model.

As it goes, the extended A/C model, or Reformed epistemology, is based on the foundation that belief in God needs no prior proof as it is a reasonable and necessary belief ("properly basic") because of the innate perception of God that humanity has. The apologist then deals with any reasonable objections to God's existence and, by extension, the Christian faith (this initial proposal of God or the Christian worldview varies as this general method is used by apologists from a variety of ecumenical traditions, such as Catholic, Protestant, Orthodox, etc.).

This model is predicated on Scripture passages such as Romans 1 being *true* before ever looking at the argument for the Christian belief. Like "*the sheep hear His voice*" method, a shortcoming of Reformed epistemology is that it starts with a passage that is presumed true while neglecting the whole of Scripture.

As we know from Romans 1, there's an innate yearning for the knowledge of God in all of us, what Calvin called the *sensus divinitatis. According to this model, we* therefore "*occasion*" *(*can have an innate sense of God's

6. "Reformed" meaning the connection to the Protestant Reformation of the 16th Century and the system of beliefs of Reformed theology (such as the sovereignty of God, the authority of Scripture, and salvation by grace alone, through faith alone, in Christ alone, and so on).
7. Alvin Plantinga, *Warranted Christian Belief*, Oxford University Press, Oxford, England, 2000, pp. 167–198.

existence) that God exists when experiencing creation, in contrast to *concluding* that God exists (as with the classical and evidential models).

In summary, with this method you assume the existence of God right from the start based on your capacity to know God exists via natural revelation (which means observing the world), and if your opponent has no real objection, then your position is true.

As author Brian Morley puts it, "So according to foundationalism, some things are known without support from other beliefs, while other things are known because we conclude them from other beliefs."8 So instead of standing on God's authoritative Word as the *ultimate predicated* belief, Reformed epistemology utilizes a concept in Romans 1 and takes that as *a priori* (the starting point).

If you're struggling to follow all this, you aren't alone! That is a flaw with the method, it has a depth that many struggle to follow. And there are a few other problems with it too:

- If the truthfulness of the Bible (a warranted Christian belief), hasn't been established yet, how do you know that Romans 1 is true?
- Where do the ideas of logic, truth, and knowledge come from in the first place? And how do we know they are unchanging, universal, and absolute? Yes, to even begin to evaluate any challenge to the proposition of Christian truth, logic must have an objective basis. So, in the end, Reformed epistemology is forced to fall back to arbitrary human logic, disconnected from the Bible, as the ultimate authority (but I'm sure these apologists believe the Bible to be true, they are just inconsistent).

So, here's the real question: Why not take all of Scripture as *a priori* true instead of just Romans 1? With all of Scripture, you have an objective basis for logic, truth, and knowledge! With that starting point, we can then see these instances of "*occasions* of God" when we interact with His creation as a confirmation of what we already expected—that God exists and His Word is true.

This model does take a type of hard stance, which is good, but it doesn't go back far enough to the ultimate presupposition—God's Word. And that's why it falls short—due to an arbitrarily picked starting point.

8. Brian Morley, *Mapping Apologetics*, IVP Academic, Downers Grove, Illinois, 2015, p. 122.

Cumulative Case

"It all adds up to God."

The cumulative case for God is not itself a "model." Instead, it uses several previously discussed models (not the presuppositional one), putting them all together to argue for the existence of God.

A cumulative case apologist takes arguments like grand design, first cause, or even evidential arguments (based on science or archaeology), and puts them together to make a *cumulative* case that God exists. But as we've previously discussed, the core problem with each of these models is that they're all *probabilistic* for the existence of God. Because none of them are absolute, they all fail. Any final solution in a cumulative case would still not be *100% sure* that God exists.

It's the same problem: they're not starting with God's Word as the absolute. They start their thinking with man's word—which undercuts the methods anyway! Of course, design, science, or archaeology evidences aren't bad in and of themselves, but, like the classical and evidential methods on which it's based, the cumulative case uses them improperly as an authority "greater" than God and His Word.

As Christians who submit to the authority of God's Word, let's humble ourselves and let God be the ultimate authority that He is. Then, put the evidence and arguments in their rightful place as *confirmations* (not "proofs") of what we expect in light of the truth of God's Word.

8 Van Til – Who Was He and What Did He Do?

> It is Christ as God who speaks in the Bible. Therefore, the Bible does not appeal to human reason as ultimate in order to justify what it says. It comes to the human being with absolute authority. Its claim is that human reason must itself be taken in the sense in which Scripture takes it, namely, as created by God and as therefore properly subject to the authority of God.[1]
> –Cornelius Van Til

Everyone knows the names of philosophers and thinkers of the past like Socrates, Plato, Aristotle, Thomas Aquinas, Nietzsche, René Descartes, Confucius, Augustine, and Charles Darwin—and they should also know the name Dr. Cornelius Van Til. He was the driving force to change the entire field of philosophy—and his impact is still sending ripples down through our current age.

Dr. Van Til was a Dutch-American philosopher and theologian (1895-1987) who taught at *Westminster Theological Seminary* for 43 years and

1. Cornelius Van Til, *A Christian Theory of Knowledge*, Presbyterian & Reformed Publishing, Phillipsburg, New Jersey, 1969, p. 15.

pastored from 1930 until he died in 1987. His philosophy for the presuppositional apologetic method lit a fire that has lived on through apologists like Dr. Greg Bahnsen (who continued his work) and the Bahnsen Institute (founded by Graham Dugas), Ken Gentry, Michael Butler, Jason Lisle and the *Biblical Science Institute*, John Frame, Jay Lucas, James White, and even the ministry of *Answers in Genesis*, the *Ark Encounter*, and the *Creation Museum*, along with many others.

I mentioned this earlier in the book but to highlight Van Til's impact, consider the case of Dr. Gordon Stein vs. Van Til's prized student, Dr. Greg Bahnsen, during The Great Debate. If I were to go up to a random atheist on the street and ask him who Gordon Stein is, he would likely have never heard of him. A few old-school atheists might remember him but his name has largely gone off into extinction among atheists—and yet Gordon Stein was arguably one of the most famous atheistic philosophers, next to Dr. Richard Dawkins, of his time.

Stein actively challenged many (classical-based) Christians on the existence of God—and usually won! He also wrote and edited many books on atheism (e.g., *The Encyclopedia of Unbelief, An Anthology of Atheism and Rationalism,* and *A Second Anthology of Atheism and the Rationalism*).

But his fame suddenly came to an end after his debate with Dr. Greg Bahnsen, the leading proponent of Van Tillian philosophy who put this philosophy to work in that debate. Gordon Stein was left stumbling over his words and, to his dying day, failed to provide an actual response to the Van Tillian philosophy that Greg Bahnsen used in that debate. Stein's legacy plummeted to where today, atheists rarely even know his name.

So, what exactly did Van Til come up with that Greg Bahnsen used so effectively? Dr. John Frame (who was similar in philosophy to Van Til but has his nuances) once said of Van Til's method:

> "Unoriginal as his doctrinal formulations may be, his use of those formulations – his application of them – is often quite remarkable. The sovereignty of God becomes an epistemological, as well as a religious and metaphysical principle."[2]

Frame is pointing out that Van Til's ideas were nothing original but his use of it was powerful in all the right ways (providing a rational basis for

2. John Frame, *Van Til the Theologian*, Pilgrim Publishing Co. Phillipsburg, New Jersey, 1976.

the necessary *preconditions of intelligibility*, which we covered in previous chapters). So where did these ideas originate? *God's Word*. Pause for a moment and consider this.

You might be thinking, "Well, of course, Christians are *supposed* to be using God's Word." That may seem obvious but many Christians just don't quite grasp the weight of the fact that the Bible is the authoritative Word of God!

You see, Van Til asked a very simple question, which is so simple that many Christians just fly by it: Why are Christian philosophers giving up the Bible and using the *same* apologetic methods that non-Christian philosophers (even pagan ones!) use to develop their philosophies?

By and large, Christian philosophers of the past and present usually gave up God and His Word when it came to philosophy and apologetic methods, even if they didn't do that in their heart. They didn't treat God and His Word like the ultimate authority that it is. Instead, they treated it as if it were not an authority at all. In other words, these Christian philosophers worshipped God as if He *absolutely* exists (like at church or during Bible study, for instance) and yet they essentially started their entire apologetic debate over God and His Word assuming God *doesn't* exist and that His Word has no authority.

Yes, Christians tossed God's Word aside and moved over to the same methods the ancient Greeks and others used historically. They assumed human logic—which didn't exist until God created humanity—is supreme over God and His Word.

In keeping with Greek thought, they further assumed that man is perfectly "neutral" and not biased in his thinking (which is a myth!). In other words, many Christians do apologetics assuming sin hasn't affected man, ignoring the biblical truth that the mind of man has been twisted and corrupted due to sin.

Van Til seemed to think that Christian philosophers would be eager to say, "Wow, that's a good idea! Let's start using the Bible as the authority that it is!" Instead, regrettably, so many Christian philosophers *opposed* him, insisting that the Bible be left out of the subject and that we should keep doing philosophy the way the Greeks did.

In other words, these *Christian* philosophers—who are supposed to be committed to God and His Word as their authority in *all* areas of life—

decided that it's best *not* to stand on biblical authority in the area of apologetics! How very sad!

Now, the reasons for the rejection of his ideas is more complicated than just that:

- He was writing in the backdrop of Dutch and German idealism. German idealism was based on Immanuel Kant's philosophy (and post-Kantian philosophers) who tried to merge *rationalism* (reason is the test of knowledge) and *empiricism* (true knowledge only comes from senses) together. Much of what Van Til wrote was to counter that philosophy, and so his writing is often tough to follow unless you were immersed in that debate.
- He was known to critique many different theological persuasions too and, consequently, he immediately turned off several Christian philosophers to his apologetic methodology.

Nevertheless, Van Til simply went back to the Bible and asked, "How does God do apologetics and philosophy?" Then he mimicked what God does in the Bible, which became known as *presuppositional* or *transcendental apologetics*. And it is powerful—which really shouldn't surprise us because the Bible is God's Word! (Who would have thought that our omniscient God knows better than us about philosophy and apologetics?!)

Consider the audacity of someone opposing the absolute authority of our omniscient, omnipresent, omnipotent God—Christians really should know better (one cannot serve two masters!). So what was the reaction among Van Til's fellow Christians and from Christians today? In summary, there have been three general responses:

1. Some opposed Van Til, of course. (I still find it hard to understand how these Christians can justify their presumption that our omniscient God shouldn't be consulted regarding philosophy and apologetics!)
2. Some really liked a lot of his ideas, and even utilized them, but overall weren't entirely convinced so they created their own deviations of it (e.g., Gordon Clark, Francis Schaeffer, Edward John Carnell).
3. Some embraced it and, praise God, we're seeing this methodology spread like wildfire today.

It reminds me of the same three general responses that Paul received at Mars Hill (the Areopagus) in Athens, Greece in Acts 17: (1) Some mocked, (2) some wanted to hear more about it but were not entirely convinced, and (3) others joined him and believed (Acts 17:32–34[3]).

At the time, did people really know that what Paul presented was devastating to all the false philosophies of Greece (e.g., idol worship, Epicureanism which is evolutionism, Stoicism, etc.)?

Do people in our era realize that Van Til did something akin to this by simply going back to God's Word for philosophy and apologetics? In the same way Paul treated the Bible as the authority amidst philosophers who didn't, so Van Til was using the Bible as the authority amidst philosophers who didn't.

3. And when they heard of the resurrection of the dead, some mocked, while others said, "We will hear you again on this matter." So Paul departed from among them. However, some men joined him and believed, among them Dionysius the Areopagite, a woman named Damaris, and others with them. (Acts 17:32–34)

The Powerful Transcendental Argument for the Existence of God

So what does starting with God's Word, instead of human reasoning, actually look like as you share your faith and "argue" with unbelievers?

The heart of the issue of the existence of God and the truth of His Word is formally known as the *Transcendental Argument for the Existence of God* (abbreviated as TAG).

This fully *biblical* apologetic method starts and ends ONLY with the God of the Bible as the absolute authority in all matters, and the knowledge that His revealed Word to man comes with the authority of God Himself.

TAG keeps God as the standard throughout the entire argument—there's no need for a blind leap of faith to the God of the Bible from some generic god! In other words, there's *never* a time in the argument where the apologist must "step off" God's Word as the ultimate standard.

The Matter of Authority

As we've already seen, the opening of the Bible treats God as the ultimate and final authority:

> *In the beginning, God created the heavens and the earth.*
> (Genesis 1:1)

When God states His existence in the first line of the Bible, He could only do it by final authority. Why? Because there is no authority greater than God. By way of revelation to man, the absolutely true God revealed His existence.

God also made His existence known in the heart of all by their conscience (e.g., Romans 1:18–32, 2:14–16[1]). As I shared in a previous chapter, unbelievers don't just know some general deity in their "heart-of-hearts"—rather they know the *true* God of the Bible but suppress this knowledge by their unrighteousness. Those who suppress the knowledge of God are given over to a debased mind (per Romans 1) and taken captive by Satan (2 Timothy 2:25–26[2]).

This means those who object to God's absolute authority are clearly not in their right mind! By what authority can someone object to God's absolute authority? The audacity of such a person shows the lack of basic logic and reason. Of course, this is not to say unbelievers are unintelligent (that's obviously untrue), but that they fail next to God who is the basis for all reason, logic, knowledge, wisdom, intelligence, and truth.

The issue of authority is ever-present in TAG (that's why we keep coming back to it!). Again, it is not like the classical or evidential arguments. Not at all. In fact, the TAG method is not really a method—rather, it is the basis for what makes *argumentation even possible in the first place!*

Some Christians mistakenly believe all the different arguments for God's existence (grand design, first cause, etc.) are like different tools in your

1. For when Gentiles, who do not have the law, by nature do the things in the law, these, although not having the law, are a law to themselves, who show the work of the law written in their hearts, their conscience also bearing witness, and between themselves their thoughts accusing or else excusing them) in the day when God will judge the secrets of men by Jesus Christ, according to my gospel. (Romans 2:14–16)
2. In humility correcting those who are in opposition, if God perhaps will grant them repentance, so that they may know the truth, and that they may come to their senses and escape the snare of the devil, having been taken captive by him to do his will. (2 Timothy 2:25–26)

apologetic “toolbox” to be used for different situations, and that you can simply throw in TAG as just another tool to grab when you need it. But if someone believes this, it shows they don’t understand the basic premise of the transcendental argument.

The transcendental argument is that, without the God of the Bible, there is no *basis* to make an argument at all! Recall that only the *biblical* worldview as revealed in Scripture provides a rational basis for the *preconditions of intelligibility*. Thus, all other man-made worldviews, since they do *not* start with God and His Word, fail right from the start. TAG is intricately connected to the authority of the God of the Bible alone. If you can wrap your mind around that vital point, you’ll have a good grasp on this method.

What Is the TAG?

TAG is *the basis from where all argumentation* can begin and be sustained.

The Bible says wisdom and knowledge begin with the fear of the Lord who has all wisdom (omnisapience) and all knowledge (omniscience)

- *The fear of the LORD is the beginning of knowledge, But fools despise wisdom and instruction* (Proverbs 1:7).
- *In whom are hidden all the treasures of wisdom and knowledge* (Colossians 2:3).

In other words, if you reject God, you’re reduced to foolishness and absurdity. If someone one responds to your use of the Bible by saying, “you can’t use the Bible since you haven’t shown the Bible is true or that God exists,” then they have already missed the power of the argument. The Bible must be predicated for *meaning, objections, argumentation, logic, knowledge, and truth* to exist in the first place.

Simply put, the truth of the Bible must be the foundation. Otherwise, you couldn’t know anything at all. And yet, ironically, the unbeliever (inconsistent to his worldview) makes *knowledge claims* that are against the Bible! For instance, when an unbeliever says, “I can’t trust the Bible because of X, Y, and Z,” he is making knowledge and truth claims without a basis for knowledge or truth.

You see, even the concept of an *objection* is predicated on the Bible being true! For someone to object to the Bible, he must *borrow* from the truthfulness of the Bible to make his objection! And he's assuming he (as a fallible creature) is in a position of authority *above* the all-knowing, all-powerful, all-present Creator God!

The objector is being arbitrary when he wants everyone to accept his authority as supreme (without question!) while at the same time objecting to God, who is the actual supreme authority. If an apologist wanted to take this to a whole other level, he could easily reverse the objector's same argument right back at him, "*You* can't use any of *your* arguments because *you* haven't been proven true or provided a basis for truth." (Note the power of a presuppositional thrust!)

But, as Christian apologists, I suggest being kinder in our response or approach! A good, proper response, considering TAG, could be something like, "I'm glad you believe the biblical principles that truth and argumentation exist, but you are giving up your worldview to borrow from God when you do this."

For someone to object, he *must* give up his worldview and assume the Bible is true for truth, logic, knowledge, love, and so on to exist. Of course, when they do this, unbelievers almost always don't realize what they've just done, so you'll likely have to point it out at least a few times, in a few different ways—kindly and respectfully, of course. But when they object, they are essentially acknowledging that their worldview fails.

And it's not just an atheistic worldview that fails. We've covered this ground already in previous chapters, but it bears repeating: every worldview *outside* of biblical Christianity fails to truly provide a basis for logic, knowledge, truth, science, morality, and so on because they are all ultimately based on man's (not God's) word.

All man-made religions, worldviews, cults, and philosophical systems can be broken into four general categories (for extensive details, see *World Religions and Cults*, a three-volume set by Master Books). These four categories are:

1. Spirit-only systems (Eastern Mysticism/monism – all is one and all is spirit)
2. Material-only systems (secular/atheistic/materialistic religions)
3. Moralistic religions (just arbitrarily follow a moral code like Confucianism, Buddhism, Wicca, mythologies, etc.)
4. Counterfeits of Christianity (such as Judaism, Islam, Latter-Day Saints [Mormons], Jehovah's Witnesses, and so on).

The four religious styles must subtly or openly borrow many things from the Bible. Consider our existence: can any Eastern mysticism religion (such as Hinduism) account for our existence? Since "all is one," then that means existing and not existing are *one* and the same. So even the truth of our existence doesn't make sense given that worldview!

Or what about the "material-only systems" like atheism, agnosticism, naturalism, evolutionism, and so on? They cannot account for, say, the laws of nature because natural laws are *immaterial*. Thus, if they are consistent with their materialistic beliefs, then natural laws can't exist and we can't do the very science they revere so much!

Moralistic religions don't have an authoritative revelation from their god, gods, or no god system, which means they have no *objective* standard for why they need to adhere to their arbitrary moral code in the first place. This defeats the purpose of morality in their religions as their ultimately subjective beliefs can change with any given person and at any given time.

Counterfeits of Christianity do something a bit different than these others. They *openly* borrow from the Bible for logic, morality, truth, and so on. They just want to add to or subtract from Scripture, or heavily reinterpret it, thus severely compromising the Word of God. But in doing so, they unwittingly reveal that the Bible is the authority, and their additions to or removals from the Scriptures are without warrant and are to be judged as errant by previous Scripture.

Yes, all other religions fall short of giving a *basis* for the very things they argue for. Simply put, they must borrow from the Bible just to argue against it; therefore, these other views are false. (These other religions will be discussed in more detail in a following chapter.)

How We Do We Know the Bible Is True?

Let's apply TAG to this fundamental question, "How do we know the Bible is true?"

It's simple: the Bible is true because any alternative would make things like knowledge, logic, and truth impossible. The Bible is the only book that has the preconditions for intelligibility. God (and subsequently His Word) is the supreme standard that makes provability possible. There is no greater standard.

Other worldviews can't claim this for their religious writings because they all must borrow from the Bible for the world to make sense as science, morality, and logic all stem from the Bible being true. If the Bible were not true, then knowledge would be impossible. In other words, if the Bible were not true, nothing would make sense—good or bad. Everything in the entire universe (material or immaterial) would be meaningless and pointless.

But, you might be wondering, if the preconditions for intelligibility depend on the truthfulness of the Bible, then how do unbelievers, who don't believe the Bible is true, still use logic and know things? Well, someone doesn't have to believe the Bible is true to use these things, but it has to be true in order for us to do science, use logic, and have knowledge of right and wrong.

Consider someone who says he doesn't believe air exists. He makes convincing verbal arguments and openly says he doesn't believe in air, all the while using air to breathe and speak his argument. It is like this with the critics of the Bible. They argue the Bible is not true and that they have knowledge to say so, all the while borrowing from the Bible, which accounts for truth and knowledge.

Think of it this way: Unless the Bible is true, which accounts for

1. knowledge,
2. truth existing,
3. and that we are made in the image of an all-knowing, logical, God of truth so we can seek and have the ability to understand the answer,

then no one and no worldview can even begin to answer the question, "How do we know the Bible is true?" unless they use these attributes from God's Word!

So when a Bible critic asks you this question, you can just respond (gently, of course) by saying, "How do you know anything is true?" and thus make him defend his position on how knowledge is even possible given his own worldview. (Spoiler alert: He will fail to give a coherent answer because there is no foundation for it!)

This is the presuppositional or transcendental argument in a nutshell: the Bible must be true for provability to be possible.

As you may have noticed, TAG has the existence of God and the absolute truth of the Bible interconnected as one. Because one is correct, the other is as well. In other words, the Bible is true, therefore the God of the Bible exists. Or vice versa, the God of the Bible exists, therefore His revealed Word to us is true. So, the transcendental argument isn't just about God's existence but about the truthfulness of the whole of Scripture. Arguing one is arguing the other.

This is what happens when you are dealing with the absolute starting point of God. His Word comes with the authority of God Himself. There is no greater starting point than God. Any lesser starting point is an attempt to demote God from His absolute position of supreme authority.

TAG Really Is Powerful

The Transcendental Argument for the Existence of God is that the God of the Bible is the basis for allowing all argumentation to proceed. In summary:

- Because the God of truth exists, truth exists.
- Because the God of love exists, love exists.
- Because the logical and reasoning God exists, logic and reasoning exists.
- Because the all-knowing God exists, knowledge exists.

And being made in the image of our all-knowing, logical God of truth and love gives us the ability to recognize truth, logic, knowledge, and so on. In TAG, God exists and His Word is predicated as true just to begin any argument, debate, proof, and so on. In negative terms, if the God of the Bible did not exist and His Word wasn't true, then it would be impossible to know or prove anything at all. Greg Bahnsen once wrote:

> What is the presuppositional starting point? Here the Christian apologist, defending his ultimate presuppositions, must be prepared to argue the ***impossibility of the contrary*** – that is, to argue that the philosophic perspective of the unbeliever destroys meaning, intelligence, and the very possibility of knowledge, while the Christian faith provides the only framework and conditions for the intelligible experience and rational certainty. The apologist must contend that the true starting point of thought *cannot be other than* God and His revealed word, for no reasoning is possible apart from that ultimate authority. Here and only here does one find the genuinely unquestionable starting point[3] (emphasis in original).

So, by the impossibility of the contrary, the Bible is true and the God of the Bible exists.

3. Greg Bahnsen, *Always Ready*, Covenant Media Press, Nocogdoches, Texas, Sixth Printing, 1996, pp. 72–73.

Neutrality vs. Common Ground

> "You can't use the Bible because I don't believe it!"

Have you ever been asked to "leave the Bible out of it" when discussing a subject, like the existence of God? Maybe you've heard something like,

> "I don't accept the Bible as the truth, so prove your God exists without using the Bible!"

Or

> "Let's discuss this, but since I don't trust the Bible, you have to use different sources, so we can meet on neutral ground."

This idea of supposed "neutrality" is nothing more than a subtle, deceitful tactic to get the apologist to throw out the Bible and have a "civilized" discussion about a topic, without all that supposed "religious stuff." But there is actually no neutral position—that's a myth. (It's technically called the *pretended neutrality fallacy*.) The Bible makes it clear that the sinner's heart is depraved, and we are either for Christ or against Him.

- He who is not with Me is against Me, and he who does not gather with Me scatters abroad (Matthew 12:30).
- Because the carnal mind is enmity against God; for it is not subject to the law of God, nor indeed can be (Romans 8:7).
- Adulterers and adulteresses! Do you not know that friendship with the world is enmity with God? Whoever therefore wants to be a friend of the world makes himself an enemy of God (James 4:4).

Whether he realizes it or not, the critic is trying to get you to give up the Bible as your ultimate authority (your starting point) and trust his starting point (*man*'s word). So he's essentially trying to get you to act like a secularist! And if you do this, you've *lost* the debate right from the start.

Consider this analogy: You see a person who is taking an illegal drug, like cocaine. As an apologist, you want to inform this person of the addictive problems associated with drug use and plead with him to stop and get help (e.g., 1 Corinthians 6:12[1]). In response to your plea he says, "Listen, we can talk about this, but first you need to do this cocaine with me." Would you do it? Of course not. You don't give up your morality based on the Bible's authority and accept his, so why give up the Bible's authority in any other area?[2]

Make sure you're on the lookout for this myth of "neutrality" in any debate. (It's a really common tactic so be ready!) Again, there is *no such thing* as neutrality! We don't want to get caught "giving up the Bible" to meet on non-existent neutral ground, otherwise the non-Christians win by default!

This is because, by getting you to "leave the Bible out of the debate" (toss it aside), you're now, by default, debating on the terms that man's opinions is the ultimate authority. Think about it: If the Bible is left out, then God is left out, which puts man in God's place as the ultimate authority. In other words, they want you to give up your starting point of God's Word and replace it with their starting point of man's word, so they win!

If it's your first time hearing something like this and you're feeling a bit confused, don't worry. The following images will hopefully help illustrate this point for you:

---

1. All things are lawful for me, but all things are not helpful. All things are lawful for me, but I will not be brought under the power of any. (1 Corinthians 6:12)
2. No analogy is perfect, and this is *not* to make light of the seriousness of drug addiction, but hopefully this gets the point across.

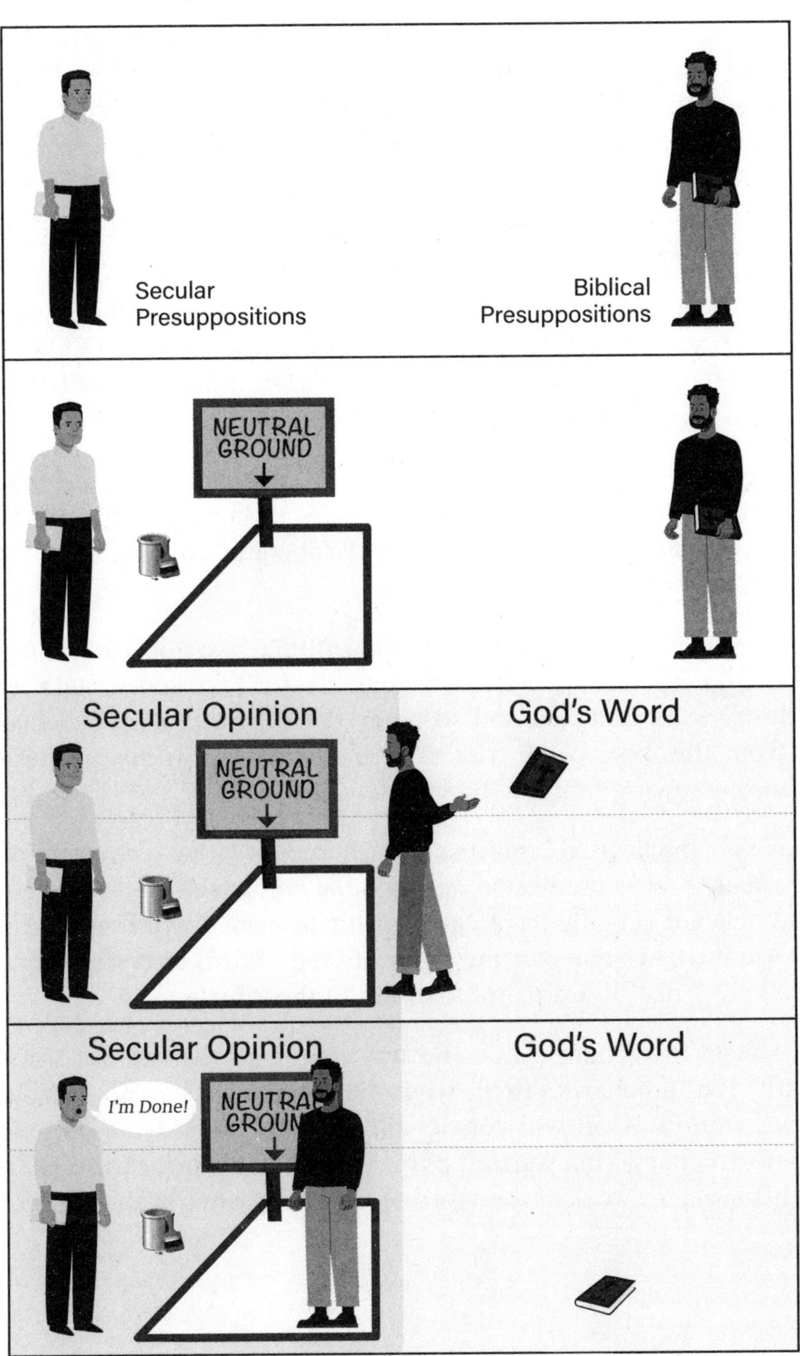
Secular
Presuppositions
Biblical
Presuppositions
NEUTRAL
GROUND
Secular Opinion
God's Word
NEUTRAL
GROUND
Secular Opinion
God's Word
I'm Done!
NEUTRA
GROUN

Although there is no *neutral* ground, there is *common* ground between believers and unbelievers. How do we find this common ground? It's easier than you think. For example, the unbeliever (likely) doesn't want to be shot and killed or lied to or stolen from. In fact, the unbeliever will often emphatically repeat that it is wrong to lie, murder, and so on. This is common ground. We don't want to be shot or lied to either! But did you catch what he's subtly doing?

He's "stepping away" from his foundation (built on man's word) and sneaking over to the biblical foundation, *borrowing* from the Bible to make his moral claims. In other words, he's *stealing* morality that doesn't belong to him, and this is what we need to point out!

So that means there is common ground, but it is *borrowed* ground that both you and the unbeliever are standing on! And the best way to point this out is by continually *pointing at his feet!* (Of course, not literally, but rather figuratively speaking.)

Make it clear (gently) to the unbeliever that things like not being murdered or lied to (morality), along with logic, truth, knowledge, science, love, clothing, work and rest, and so on are all *Christian doctrines* that emanate from the Bible being true. And if he believes in *any* of these things—he's borrowing from the Bible!

Just to have an intellectual conversation where words have any sort of meaning whatsoever is predicated on the Bible being true. So, by necessity, the unbeliever actually has to give up his professed worldview/religion and use the Christian starting point of God's Word to discuss anything—including his futile attempt to discredit the Bible!

Apologists need to recognize this and use it to "pull the rug out from underneath" the unbeliever. Then, when he realizes he has no reliable foundation, we pray God will convict him to step aboard the biblical foundation—to change his starting point (which is a work of the Holy Spirit on his heart—a work of the Word of God that convicts and saves).

Christian
Presuppositions
Christian
Presuppositions
Secular
Presuppositions
Christian
Presuppositions
Secular
Presuppositions
Christian
Presuppositions

Actually, when unbelievers borrow from the Christian starting point (the Bible) in order to attack the Bible, they are essentially "blowing themselves up" too—whether they realize it or not. Hence, their position is self-refuting. For instance, suppose the unbeliever says, "Here's an argument that demonstrates the Bible is wrong..." but did you catch that the fact that he can even *argue at all* demonstrates that he's wrong because if he tries to discredit the Bible, then he loses the foundation for argumentation itself?

When we meet on common ground, it's critically important to point out to the unbeliever that he is actually standing on borrowed ground—God's ground! (Of course, he likely won't understand this point, so you may need to explain it a few times.)

To refer back to The Great Debate, this is exactly what Greg Bahnsen did to Gordon Stein. He pointed out that for Stein to even show up for the debate and use things like logic, he must give up his atheistic/materialistic religion, which cannot account for logic—thus his worldview is false! Stein had to inconsistently borrow from the truthfulness of the Bible to even use logic to try and argue against it!

I used a similar tactic on Bill Nye, TV's "the Science Guy," during our famous debate at the Creation Museum on February 4, 2014[3] that's been watched by tens of millions around the world. During my 30-minute case I said that,

> Non-Christian scientists are really borrowing from the Christian worldview anyway to carry out their experimental observational science....When they're doing observational science using the scientific method they have to assume the laws of logic, they have to assume the laws of nature, they have to assume the uniformity of nature.

Interestingly, Nye failed to understand how devasting this is to his position—he just ignored it! (At least Stein realized how devasting it was during his debate!)

But the issue has never been about "neutral" ground. All ground belongs to God! He created all things and is the One who makes knowledge and truth possible within His creation. And no matter how hard unbelievers try to suppress it, this reality is inescapable for anyone made in God's image and living in His creation. When unbelievers want to use some of the dirt (i.e., logic, knowledge, truth, morality, science, etc.) from God's ground, we need to point out to them that it is God's ground.

No, there is no neutrality but, yes, there's common ground—God's ground!

3. Ken Ham, *Inside the Nye-Ham Debate*, Master Books, Green Forest, Arkansas, 2014, pp. 50–52.

How to Use Evidence

"But what about the evidence?"

Let's deal with a common misconception about presuppositional apologetics: that we don't use evidence. This is simply not true—just go to our website! Answers in Genesis is a presuppositional apologetics ministry and yet our website is full of articles detailing the evidence that confirms the truth of God's Word. Yes, we use evidence all the time! But the difference is *how* we use the evidence.

Evidential or classical apologetics, as we've seen, uses the evidence to try to "prove" the possibility of some general existence of a "god"; presuppositional apologetics uses evidence as a confirmation of what we expect to find because the Bible is true.

Some of the uses of evidence are:

1. Confirming a biblical worldview,
2. Introduction to worldviews,

3. Showing inconsistencies and arbitrariness in false worldviews,
4. Showing unbelievers they must use the Bible to properly understand evidence.

Let's look at an example for each of these four purposes.

Confirming a Biblical Worldview

We often come across evidence that is a great confirmation of the Bible's truthfulness. One excellent example is the global flood of Noah's day (Genesis 6–9).

As I say in my presentations, if there really was a global flood, what would you expect to find? Billions of dead things buried in rock layers laid down by water all over the earth. And that's exactly what we do find! It's a confirmation of what we would expect to see as a result of the global flood.

Billions of dead things buried in rock layers laid down by water all over the earth

Or consider DNA, the molecule of heredity. We know information only comes from other information (that's what we observe) and DNA really is a complex language system. It's a confirmation of exactly what we'd expect if there is a Creator God.

We can use evidence like this (and there's so much more!) when discussing the Christian worldview with an unbeliever to *confirm* (not prove) that God's Word is the right starting point.

Introduction to Worldviews

Everyone loves evidence—that's why when an unbeliever and a biblical Christian engage in discussion, both are going to use evidence to argue for their position. And this can be good for the Christian apologist because they can use evidence regarding origins, for instance, to help the unbeliever realize that the debate is really about *worldviews* (and the presuppositions that make up their worldviews), not the evidence.

We all have the same evidence (the same DNA, rock layers, oceans, archaeological finds, continents, fossils, and so on), but interpret it very differently because we have different starting points and therefore different worldviews. These differing interpretations can be used to show the unbeliever that the issue is deeper than the evidence; it's a *worldview* issue! It's a battle between two different *religious* views that result in two different interpretations.

And that's where the real battle lies! Highlight this for the unbeliever by taking the evidence he presents and reinterpreting it within a biblical worldview. Then gently and respectfully point out that the real debate is actually at the level of your *starting point* (God's Word vs. man's word) and the very different worldviews that come from those starting points.

Did you see how evidence can be used as a powerful way to get people to think about the religious convictions that underlie their worldview?

Showing Inconsistencies and Arbitrariness in False Worldviews

Here's where we use evidence to go on the offensive and undermine the unbeliever's worldview by showing inconsistency within it.

For example, the evolutionary worldview teaches that dinosaurs evolved into birds over millions of years. However, a number of years ago "fully formed feathers" were found in rock layers supposedly from the "dawn" of dinosaurs' existence—"80 million years" ahead of their time![1] The response from secularists was that they only "look like feathers" so they're not actually true feathers.

Why? Because, given their worldview and evolutionary timescale, dinosaurs hadn't evolved into birds yet so they can't be feathers! (Note the utter inconsistency!)

Another example is carbon-14 (C14) which has been found throughout coal layers believed to be millions of years old and in diamonds, the hardest natural material on Earth, thought to be billions of years old. Here's the problem for those who hold to an old earth: C14 has a relatively short half-life of around 5,700 years (as measured in the lab). A half-life is how long we project (in the lab, in ideal conditions) it would take for half of a sample to decay (in this case from C14 into nitrogen). It then takes the same amount of time for the next half (a quarter of the original amount) to decay, and so on until it's gone.

Within their own worldview, C14 should be undetectable in 50,000-100,000 years. And yet we find it in coal assumed to be millions of years old and diamonds believed to be billions of years old! These findings are inconsistent with the evolutionary worldview (but what we'd expect if the earth is young, as the Bible teaches).

A common response to this objection is that there must have been an unknown (really a magical) mechanism that allowed new C14 to seep into the layers—and get right back where it originally was! But notice how arbitrary this rescuing device is! It's just an excuse to try to save a

1. Jeff Hecht, *New Scientist*, "Dinosaur Reveals Fully Formed Feathers" March 6, 2002, p. 8.

faulty worldview! (And, in the case of diamonds, that excuse won't work because the lattice crystalline structure is too tight to allow any C14 to get in!)

I used evidence this way during my debate with Bill Nye when I pointed out a piece of wood encased in a solidified lava flow. The lava flow was dated to 45 million years using potassium-argon dating (considered by secular scientists to be one of the most accurate methods). However, the wood encased in the lava was dated at only 45,000 years old using carbon dating.[2] How could a 45,000-year-old piece of wood be encased in a 45-million-year-old rock? It means there's a problem with these dating methods—and yet they are taken as "proof" of a millions-of-years-old earth. Again, here we have an utter inconsistency in the secular worldview.

And how did Nye respond to this piece of evidence? By claiming it was reasonable to assume the rock "slid on top" of the wood[3] —ignoring the fact that the wood was encased in the rock.[4] His response just showed 1) he didn't understand the evidence I'd presented and 2) his heart was hard and he wasn't actually looking for truth, he would just reinterpret whatever evidence I gave him in light of his worldview.

Nye's response to begin his rebuttal was, "Thank you, Mr. Ham, but I'm completely unsatisfied."[5] And he didn't address this evidence further.

Did you catch how the evidence can be used to show inconsistencies and arbitrariness within the unbelievers' *worldview*? This brings us back, once again, to our starting points.

To Show the Unbeliever They Must Use the Bible to Properly Understand Evidence

Finally, evidence can be used to share with the unbeliever that the very *basis* to logically think about evidence is predicated on the Bible's truthfulness! As I've said over and over—only the biblical worldview can provide an actual basis for things like knowledge, logic, correct reason, reliability of

2. Ken Ham, *Inside the Nye-Ham Debate*, Master Books, Green Forest, Arkansas, 2014, p. 157–158.
3. Ibid., p. 167–168.
4. Ibid., p. 187; (see also: Andrew Snelling, "Radioactive 'Dating' in Conflict!," *Creation*, Volume 20, Number 1 (December 1997): 24–27, https://answersingenesis.org/geology/radiometric-dating/radioactive-dating-in-conflict/).
5. Ibid., p. 192.

our senses, minds that can understand the world, and so on—all of which are *required* to make sense of the evidence.

In other words, we can't even begin to properly understand logic, let alone have a logical understanding of the evidence we're looking at, unless the Bible is true. By starting with the Bible, not only can we make sense of the evidence, but we have the basis on which to do so. This is one of the most powerful uses of evidence because it goes right to the heart of the problem for unbelievers.

And it's not just atheists and materialists (or other secular views) that have this problem. When discussing evidence with Eastern mystics (think Hinduism, New Age, or Taoism), if the person is consistent with their worldview of monism ("all is one," "all is spirit"), they don't really believe that anything *material* exists but that anything material is an illusion (i.e., called "*maya*" in Hinduism). So, if everything is just an illusion, including their wallet, then the Hindu, New Ager, or Taoist should have no problem with simply giving you all their money! (Again, note the inconsistency!) See how evidence—even a wallet!—can be used to contradict their worldview?

Yes, presuppositionalists effectively use evidence! The problem isn't evidence; it's your starting point: man's word or God's Word.

Limitations of Evidences in Scripture

Now I want to clarify something important: evidence won't convince everyone. Many people think if they just present the unbeliever with enough, or with the right, evidence, it will convince them the Bible is true. But, as we saw in my example above with Bill Nye, that's not the case because the issue isn't really the evidence—it's a spiritual issue!

Consider that people saw the resurrected Christ and *still didn't believe*! And these doubters included Jesus' very disciples! Immediately before Jesus gives the Great Commission, prior to His ascension into Heaven to sit at the right hand of God the Father on the Throne of God, Matthew 28:16–17 says:

> *Then the eleven disciples went away into Galilee, to the mountain which Jesus had appointed for them. When they saw Him, they worshiped Him; but some doubted.*

Some doubted! They had met with, ate bread with, and conversed with the risen Savior (e.g., John 21:13–14[6]) and some still doubted! Note that the famous "doubting Thomas" was not among the "some doubted" at this point as he did believe by now (John 20:28[7]).

The body of Christ was indeed evidence of the Resurrection, but again evidence doesn't always convince someone because their worldview and sin nature still gets in the way of properly interpreting evidence—even what we think of as "rock solid" evidence, like the resurrected body of Christ!

So what ended up changing the minds of these doubting disciples? We know from the book of Acts, and church history, that they all eventually believed—and so strongly believed they were willing to face horrible deaths (except John, who suffered banishment) as witnesses for Christ.

Well, at Pentecost, when the Holy Spirit came upon them, *then* they had a proper understanding of the evidence. The disciples of Christ became powerful witnesses throughout the world because of the convincing power *of God*—yes, it's God who saves!

Or consider John 12:37 where Jesus was speaking with a crowd of people who have seen many of His great signs and miracles:

> *But although He had done so many signs before them, they did not believe in Him.*

The people witnessed the miracles and yet still didn't believe. Often times when you're sharing the gospel, someone will say, "well, if God would just [insert miracle here], I would believe in Him!" But you can use these Scriptures to show him or her that's not true! The problem isn't evidence; it's hard hearts.

Evidence doesn't convince; God does. And God can use that evidence to awaken people's hearts to truth which is why we should always use evidence properly interpreted in light of God's Word.

I love using evidence—you can see that in my books, articles I've written, and my presentations. As I share how genetics confirms the biblical teaching of kinds or fossils confirm the flood or DNA confirms there's only one race, I'll often ask the audience, "isn't it exciting to be a Christian?" Yes,

---

6. Jesus then came and took the bread and gave it to them, and likewise the fish. This is now the third time Jesus showed Himself to His disciples after He was raised from the dead. (John 21:13–14)
7. And Thomas answered and said to Him, "My Lord and my God!" (John 20:28)

it it! Evidence is exciting—but we must always frame it in the context of God's Word and the history He's given us (e.g. God designed things perfectly, but due to sin, things are broken; there was the global Flood; the tower of Babel event, and so on).

When we interpret the evidence in light of God's Word, we are going to do a better job of getting closer to the correct interpretation. Of course, God is always right and we, as fallible human beings, can and do make mistakes in our interpretations. But letting God be the authority when looking at evidence, keeps us accountable to align with thinking God's thoughts after Him.

12 Proof vs. Persuasion

"Why didn't I say…or why couldn't I have remembered…?"

Have you ever walked away from a witnessing encounter and thought, "Why didn't I…?" We've all done that at some point! It's going to happen so don't let it bother you.

Or maybe you've walked away from an argument and thought, "*Wow, I really do think I said everything right!*"…but the unbeliever still didn't believe or even respond positively? Again, don't let it bother you. But this brings me to the point of this chapter.

We, as Christians, can get caught up in debates over the existence of God or the Bible's truth with the mindset that, if the unbeliever doesn't change their mind and attitude toward God right there on the spot, we failed. But we can do everything "right," say all the "right" things, answer every objection perfectly, and so on, and still not see the *fruit* (a changed heart/mind) of that conversation.

Think of it like a child who goes out and plants an apple seed in the ground. With help, she prepared the soil correctly, planted the seed in a good spot with plenty of sunlight, and properly watered it. Then, a few minutes later, she asks, "Where is my tree and fruit?" The child needs to understand she missed something key: Time is required for the tree to grow and eventually produce fruit.

It's similar when we're doing apologetics and evangelism. We can say everything "right," but sometimes we miss the key factor: the Holy Spirit, God Himself working in the heart of an unbeliever.

> *Therefore I make known to you that no one speaking by the Spirit of God calls Jesus accursed, and no one can say that Jesus is Lord except by the Holy Spirit.* (1 Corinthians 12:3)

> *And a servant of the Lord must not quarrel but be gentle to all, able to teach, patient, in humility correcting those who are in opposition, if God perhaps will grant them repentance, so that they may know the truth, and that they may come to their senses and escape the snare of the devil, having been taken captive by him to do his will.* (2 Timothy 2:24–26)

The Bible makes it clear that the Holy Spirit is the One who changes hearts. In Psalm 51:10, we read that it is God who creates a clean heart within us and renews our spirit. He grants us repentance and makes it possible for us to say that "Jesus is Lord."

Far too often, Christians think it's their responsibility to change the hearts of unbelievers, failing to realize that is God's job, not ours. Only God can raise the dead to life!

> *Most assuredly, I say to you, he who hears My word and believes in Him who sent Me has everlasting life, and shall not come into judgment, but has passed from death into life.* (John 5:24)

> *We know that we have passed from death to life, because we love the brethren. He who does not love his brother abides in death.* (1 John 3:14)

It's true that men rolled away the stone that covered Lazarus' grave, but it was Jesus who brought life back into his body (John 11:38–44). It was the angels who rolled away the stone from Jesus' grave (Matthew 28:2–4[1]), but it was Jesus (who is God) who raised Himself to life.

> *Therefore My Father loves Me, because I lay down My life that I may take it again. No one takes it from Me, but I lay it down of Myself. I have power to lay it down, and I have power to take it again. This command I have received from My Father.* (John 10:17–18)

This is why we can (1) completely dismantle the unbelievers' worldview, (2) shooting down every argument the unbeliever has against God and His Word. Then (3) present the truth of the biblical worldview (including *why the Bible is true and why God exists*) along with (4) the gospel—and yet, be met with scoffing and unbelief. It's the difference between *proof and persuasion*. We can "prove" the biblical position, but we cannot persuade unbelievers to believe it.

It's God's job, working in their hears, to change the innermost beliefs of unbelievers. As apologists, we are to refute false views, present the truth of Scripture and the gospel (the good news of Jesus' life, death, burial, and resurrection), and show how they are suppressing the knowledge of God.

We are to "roll away the stone," but it is the job of the Holy Spirit to bring them to repentance (2 Timothy 2:25[2]) and to persuade them to the saving knowledge of Christ.

Of course, there are times when unbelievers *do* have a change of heart/mind right there on the spot after you briefly share truth with them—and praise God! But that's usually because another Christian before you first planted the seed and then another Christian came and watered it, but it is always God who gives the growth, and you were just the believer God sovereignly chose to see the fruit of that conversion (1 Corinthians 3:5–9).

Practical Example

Here's a practical example a fellow apologist once shared with me. He was once teaching an apologetics course at his local church. Before the class

1. And behold, there was a great earthquake; for an angel of the Lord descended from heaven, and came and rolled back the stone from the door, and sat on it. His countenance was like lightning, and his clothing as white as snow. And the guards shook for fear of him, and became like dead men. (Matthew 28:2-4)
2. In humility correcting those who are in opposition, if God perhaps will grant them repentance, so that they may know the truth. (2 Timothy 2:25)

started, he was informed that an atheist—the husband of a Christian at his church—was going to come.

Instead of "walking on eggshells" (as many apologists would've done), he decided to deal with the obvious problem right up front by thoroughly disproving atheism in the very first class. (We'll expand on this disproof of atheism in the next chapter.)

He said that half of the attendees were nervously waiting for fireworks to erupt at the end of class! But something else happened. That atheist came up afterward and said, "That grabbed my attention. I'll be back for the rest of the classes." And he did—even bringing a folder for notes and my friend's handouts. After the class ended, the atheist never really shared his thoughts, and the apologist ended up moving to a different state.

But, after a few months had passed, my friend's phone lit up with calls from people at his old church sharing excitedly that this atheist was now *saved* and, in obedience to Christ, had made a public profession of faith and had been baptized. His testimony included that very class which he said had "convinced my mind but not my heart." He shared that he'd wrestled with himself over this for some time "but finally the Holy Spirit convinced my heart." He repented and was saved. What a wonderful testimony of God's word!

As this example shows, an apologist can answer questions based on biblical authority and present the gospel (the "proof"), but it is the Holy Spirit who does the real work of salvation by converting unbelievers into believers in Christ's death, burial, and resurrection (the persuasion).

13 The Disproof of Atheism

So how do you disprove atheism? Well, to understand that, you first need to understand the religion of atheism.

Atheism is a *religion* (yes, you read that correctly!) built on the idea that they "know" *there is no God.* Note, this is not to be confused, as it often is, with the religion of *agnosticism.* Agnosticism[1] is a religion that says "*you can't know if God exists or not.*" It's sometimes called "soft atheism" because, in practice, the agnostic lives like an atheist.

Here I'm talking about *true* atheism—the religious faith that makes an absolute statement that God does not exist. It is an absolute religion, but this belief system is built on a few other things too, primarily the religious beliefs of naturalism and materialism.

1. The term "agnostic" means "without knowledge" and, thus claims, "I can't know if God exists" or something similar. However, this is actually a self-refuting position! Think about it: How can the agnostic be ***certain*** if that claim itself is actually certain? In other words, how do you really ***know*** that you can't know if God exists? (Notice how the agnostic must make a knowledge claim to "prove" that he has no knowledge about God!)

Naturalism is the belief that nature (i.e., the universe) is all that exists (as opposed to *supernaturalism* where supernatural beings, like the God of the Bible [John 4:24[2]] and His angels [Hebrews 1:13–14[3]], can exist).

Naturalists, who are by definition atheists, *cannot* leave open the possibility of anything existing *outside* of nature because of their hard stance on the supernatural (i.e., God) not existing. In other words, if the atheist left open the concept of the supernatural, they wouldn't be an atheist anymore because God *could* exist there.

M*aterialism* is the religious view that underpins the atheistic and naturalistic worldview. In materialism, only matter/energy exist within the natural universe (i.e., no spiritual realm, hence no God). Atheism, naturalism, and materialism are all different sides of the same coin and go "hand in hand" with each other.

Of course, God disagrees with the atheistic position and therefore, we know it is false. That's our starting point. But, with that in mind, we can actually destroy atheism *from within its own story* (i.e., *by an internal critique within the atheistic worldview*).

The Disproof of Atheism

Atheists believe there is nothing immaterial (materialism) or supernatural (naturalism), and they claim to ***know*** with 100% certainty that there is no God. So, let's evaluate this knowledge claim as if they were correct (within their own viewpoint). How did they come to this conclusion?

Have they looked for God? If so, then where? Did they look under every rock in the world? Did they look for God on the moon? Did they look for Him inside distant stars to see if He was there? Is He behind Saturn? Or maybe God was just too hard to see? After all, God could be hidden very small (the size of quarks or atoms) or camouflaged, etc.

Or worse, what if the atheist did look under a rock and didn't see God, then looked under another rock but God *had moved* and is now under the rock that the atheist already looked under. Now the atheist is in a real quandary!

2. God is Spirit, and those who worship Him must worship in spirit and truth. (John 4:24)
3. But to which of the angels has He ever said: "Sit at My right hand, Till I make Your enemies Your footstool"? Are they not all ministering spirits sent forth to minister for those who will inherit salvation? (Hebrews 1:13–14)

The atheist would have to look *everywhere* in the entire universe—at the exact *same* time—to say there was no God. But even then, that wouldn't be absolute.

Here's the point: The atheist would have to be *omnipresent (existing everywhere, all at once)* to make the claim that "there is no God." See the problem? *Being omnipresent is a trait of God!* So, the atheist is forced into the position of having to be "God" in order to say that "there is no God"—which refutes atheism.

And if the atheist says he doesn't need to waste time with such an endeavor because he already *knows* God doesn't exist, then he has yet *another* quandary since man can only accumulate a small amount of knowledge in his lifetime.

To be in a position to know whether or not God exists would require infinite knowledge for *all time*. The atheist would have to have *all* knowledge of the past, present, and future (every movement of every subatomic particle!) to really be in a position to grasp the required knowledge needed to speak to the existence of the God of the Bible.

Now the atheist doesn't just have to be *omnipresent* but also omniscient (all-knowing)! So, again, he's in an embarrassing position of having to claim to be God to make the assertion that "God doesn't exist." Therefore, the only way to say "there is no God" (within the atheist's own worldview) is to be…God. Thus, atheism is self-refuting and false.

Of course, the atheist (if he still wants to chat and hasn't walked away yet) could flip the argument around and point out that we, as Christians, don't know all things either, so we are also not in a position to know if God exists, nor have we looked everywhere at the exact same time to verify His existence. This is true. Christians aren't omnipresent or omniscient. But we don't have to be because we know *Someone* who is omnipresent and omniscience, as well as eternal and always truthful—the God of the Bible.

So, when atheists make this claim, they miss the simple point: the only one in the position to actually state God's existence is *God*. And God—who knows all things, sees everything in the universe at all time, and is the very one who created and upholds existence itself—has revealed His existence through His authoritative Word.

The atheist has no God to appeal to in order to prove His non-existence. Thus, the atheistic position is refuted and disproved.

And it gets worse when you turn to naturalism and materialism.

Atheists generally agree that knowledge exists and that we can *know* things (like their claim they "know" God doesn't exist). But knowledge isn't material! To acknowledge that knowledge exists is to deny the materialistic atheistic position! Some atheists assert that knowledge is just chemical reactions in the brain, but this response really doesn't help as it makes knowledge completely meaningless. Concepts like proof, provable, reliable senses, ideas, logic, existence, conclusions, thought, intelligence, and so on are also not *material!* The mere existence of these things is totally devastating to the materialistic atheistic perspective!

The religion of atheism is fraught with severe problems—and yet many people *still believe it!* And that's because, as we've discussed in previous chapters, the minds of unbelievers, according to God's Word, are corrupt and cannot think properly. And unless God intervenes and opens their eyes so they can think correctly, they will remain in that state. But praise God that He really is all-powerful (omnipotent) and He does save atheists every day.

Salvation is possible for even the most aggressive, hostile, militant atheist in the world—which actually shows the unconditional love and care of our God. It's a reminder to always pray that those ensnared by the foolish religion of atheism will someday see through its inconsistencies and come to faith in Christ by the work of the Holy Spirit.

The Veil of a Debased Mind

Do you really understand the spiritual state of the unbeliever?

The Bible makes it clear that the unbeliever has a veil over his eyes, has a mind that suppresses the knowledge of God, and has been given over to a depraved mind. As a result, he is not just spiritually "sick" but *spiritually dead* (e.g., Ephesians 2:1[1],2:5[2]; 1 Corinthians 2:14[3])! Only the *God of life* can heal him and bring him to life.

Sin has warped the mind of man. And the only solution is to think God's perfect thoughts after Him. We're given a taste of this when we're saved and the Bible is our absolute guide to correct thinking, by the power of the Holy Spirit within us sanctifying us (i.e., making us holy, transforming us to be more like Christ and less like our old selves, e.g. 2 Corinthians

1. And you He made alive, who were dead in trespasses and sins. (Ephesians 2:1)
2. Even when we were dead in trespasses, made us alive together with Christ (by grace you have been saved). (Ephesians 2:5)
3. But the natural man does not receive the things of the Spirit of God, for they are foolishness to him; nor can he know them, because they are spiritually discerned. (1 Corinthians 2:14)

5:17[4]). But in this sin-cursed and broken world, we need to remember that the mind of an unbeliever is *blinded* and thus not able to discern spiritual things:

- *He has blinded their eyes and hardened their hearts, lest they should see with their eyes, lest they should understand with their hearts and turn, so that I should heal them.* (John 12:40)
- *But even if our gospel is veiled, it is veiled to those who are perishing, whose minds the god of this age has blinded, who do not believe, lest the light of the gospel of the glory of Christ, who is the image of God, should shine on them.* (2 Corinthians 4:3–4)
- *This I say, therefore, and testify in the Lord, that you should no longer walk as the rest of the Gentiles walk, in the futility of their mind, having their understanding darkened, being alienated from the life of God, because of the ignorance that is in them, because of the blindness of their heart; who, being past feeling, have given themselves over to lewdness, to work all uncleanness with greediness.* (Ephesians 4:17–19)
- *To the pure all things are pure, but to those who are defiled and unbelieving nothing is pure; but even their mind and conscience are defiled. They profess to know God, but in works they deny Him, being abominable, disobedient, and disqualified for every good work.* (Titus 1:15–16)
- *And a servant of the Lord must not quarrel but be gentle to all, able to teach, patient, in humility correcting those who are in opposition, if God perhaps will grant them repentance, so that they may know the truth, and that they may come to their senses and escape the snare of the devil, having been taken captive by him to do his will.* (2 Timothy 2:24–26)

And that's just a sampling of verses—we could go on (e.g. Romans 1:18–28, Romans 11:7–25, 2 Corinthians 3:7–16…)!

He Gets the Glory

As a presuppositional apologist, these passages are important to always keep in the back of your mind during witnessing encounters because they remind you of the condition of the unbeliever's mind—it's blinded to the truth. And remember that it's *only* the Holy Spirit who opens the eyes of unbelievers to grant them repentance and proper understanding.

4. Therefore, if anyone is in Christ, he is a new creation; old things have passed away; behold, all things have become new. (2 Corinthians 5:17)

The Holy Spirit can use what we say to convict unbelievers of sin and their need for repentance. But if you start thinking "what more could I have said?", don't let it bother you. The Holy Spirit can even use your imperfect, ineloquent, stumbling words, in His own timing, to do way more than you think so that God gets the glory, not us.

The Holy Spirit can and does work miracles in the sinful lives of unbelievers, even as they try to suppress the truth! This is why we should always witness using God's Word first and foremost—because it's God's Word that never comes back void and always accomplishes God's purposes (Isaiah 55:11[5]). When using God's Word, you are using *what God says* to the unbeliever.

So, one of our main goals in apologetics is to help unbelievers realize they are suppressing the truth through their sinful denial of God and His Word. The Holy Spirit can use this to open their eyes to the bankruptcy of the false beliefs that ensnare them.

Win the Person, Not Just the Argument

And don't forget that our defense of the faith must always be done with kindness, patience, gentleness, and respect. We're looking to win a person to Christ, not beat them in argument after all!

Think of it this way: Imagine you're having a discussion with a *blind* person on the sidewalk. She thinks it's safe to cross the busy intersection because she believes there are no cars on the road. Would you start shoving and furiously yelling at her regarding the truth of her situation? Or would you humbly offer to take her by the hand and gently lead her? It's the same thing when dealing with unbelievers who are *blind* to the truth. Our job as Christians is to be patient, kind, gentle, and respectful while leading them to the truth, and we pray that God uses our efforts for His glory.

Please don't miss this point! Our attitude matters to God and it matters to the unbeliever. Many times, when someone discovers these powerful apologetic weapons to contend for and defend biblical truth, effectively *stopping* the mouths of unbelievers, *he* or *she* becomes arrogant and proud—that's not the right attitude! Remember, apart from Christ

5. So shall My word be that goes forth from My mouth; It shall not return to Me void, But it shall accomplish what I please, And it shall prosper in the thing for which I sent it. (Isaiah 55:11)

awakening your heart from the dead, you would be just as trapped in sin and foolishness as the unbeliever you're conversing with. And that unbeliever is made in God's image and of invaluable worth to God—he or she deserves our respect, compassion, and Christ-like love.

Never forget that we could shoot down every argument presented by unbelievers all day long, but if we don't lead them respectfully to the saving gospel message, then we have *not* successfully defended the faith! Our ultimate goal should always be to see people *saved*, not merely to win arguments. And we should never have the desire to glorify ourselves by trying to appear "more intellectual" than the unbeliever. Rather, our desire should always be to humbly glorify God in everything we do and leave the results up to His will.

Isn't Starting with the Bible Circular Reasoning?

"Isn't it circular reasoning to start with the Bible when defending the Bible?"

This is probably the most common objection to the presuppositional apologetic method: the accusation of circular reasoning. Unfortunately, many people don't realize the intricacies of circular reasoning.

The first intricacy is that there are two different types of circular reasoning: *vicious (bad)* and *virtuous (good)*. When people think of circular reasoning, they usually think of vicious circular reasoning (meaning it is arbitrary and, thus, *"not sound"*).

The second intricacy is that circular reasoning is actually *valid* in logic and reasoning—that probably surprises you! For a circular argument to be considered fallacious (or arbitrary), it must not be *soun*d. Being rational means being both "valid" and "sound." If it is "valid" and "not sound," then it could be fallacious.

As a reminder from Chapter 4 on logic, an argument can be either "valid" or "invalid." If it's a valid argument, the conclusion follows from the premises. If not, it's invalid. A "sound" argument means it's a valid argument that has *true* premises and thus a *true* conclusion. So, with the case of circular reasoning, the conclusion necessarily must follow from the premise, which means, by definition, that circular reasoning is *valid* (but still could be not sound).

So what about this claim that presuppositional apologists are just talking in circles regarding the existence of God and the truthfulness of His revealed Word? Well, critics usually fail to realize there are two forms of circular reasoning. They erroneously assume that *all* circular reasoning is the arbitrary form (*vicious* circular reasoning) and thus miss the important second form that is non-arbitrary (*absolute* circular reasoning or *virtuous* circular reasoning). Again, the arbitrary form is indeed fallacious but not the absolute form—and this is vital when dealing with the absolute starting point of God and His Word.

As previously mentioned, circular reasoning is unique because it is *valid*. It only becomes fallacious if it is not *sound*, which is due to the arbitrariness. For instance, imagine you ask someone where he lives and he responds with, "I live with my wife."

You would probably then respond with, "Okay, well, where does your wife live?"

"With me."

"Well, where do the two of you live?"

"With our kids."

"Well, where do your kids live?" (Are you exasperated yet?)

"They live with us."

This is circular. But notice that everything he said was *true*. This shows the unique nature of a circular argument. Even if it is arbitrary and unsound, it can still turn out to be true in some instances! So when I say there are intricacies of circular reasoning, I really did mean it!

But this example is still an arbitrary (not sound) argument because we never really got anywhere or answered the actual question (you still don't know where he lives!). This would be an example of a vicious (bad) circular argument.

Now let's look at the other form of circular reasoning—virtuous (good)—which is sometimes unavoidable. What if I had an interesting dream and wanted to tell you about it but you responded to my story with, "prove it logically!" I have no choice but to *appeal to myself* as the authority regarding my dream. I must start with myself to tell anyone about my dream; thus, I am appealing to myself, which is circular.

The difference is that I am the only one in a position to know my dream (other than God, of course![1]). So, although this reasoning was circular, it is virtuous (not arbitrary). There is no other possible starting point regarding the debate over my dream.

It works in a similar way with the existence of God. If God is God, then only He can reveal Himself by final and absolute authority—a *virtuous* circle. This is because God is the absolute authority on all matters—including His existence (as well as the existence of logic, knowledge, truth, love, revelation, and so on). There is *no* arbitrariness in the absolute God of the Bible. So, any allegation that states otherwise would *not* be the God of the Bible but an arbitrary (false) god, which every Christian ought to join in arguing against.

Again, the God of the Bible is not arbitrary but absolute, which means His revelation of Himself is also absolute and virtuous. Therefore, this circular reasoning is a *virtuous* circle, being both *valid and sound.*

Actually, any time you're dealing with absolutes or ultimate standards, some degree of circular reasoning is *always required.* For instance, consider trying to prove the existence of logic. To do that, you must obviously first *assume* logic exists so that you can use logic to make an argument for its existence. Critics of presuppositional apologetics, including atheists, usually misunderstand the nature of this valid and sound form of circular reasoning.

If an atheist wants to argue that you're being circular by starting with the Bible to defend the Bible, you can point out two things. One: the atheist's worldview (which, if you recall from previous chapters, comes out of naturalism and materialism) has no basis for the existence of *logic* or truth since they aren't material. So for the atheist to object to circular reasoning he must borrow from the biblical worldview!

---

1. In the Bible we see that God knew the content of Pharaoh and Nebuchadnezzar's dreams and how to interpret them (Genesis 40–41 and Daniel 2, 4).

Two: the atheist position itself is a *vicious circle*. Think about it: b*y what authority* can the atheist claim there is no God? Only by *his* own authority! When the atheist claims "there is no God," he is appealing to *his own arbitrary authority* to make such a claim—thus a circular argument. Yes, that's as circular as it gets!

Ant that's not a virtuous (good) form of circular reasoning but a vicious (bad) one because it's arbitrary since mankind is not absolute. So, atheists are actually committing a *vicious* circular argument when they claim God doesn't exist. When we dive into the intricacies of circular reasoning, God remains unscathed—but the atheistic position is left wanting.

Where Did God Come From? Or Who Created God?

I've been asked "who made God?" hundreds of times over the years. Sometimes it's a curious child, other times it's an atheist thinking it's a "gotcha!" question. But, really, it's a question with several assumptions baked into it. It assumes time is absolute and God appeared on the scene at some point. But this is not the nature of the God of the Bible.

It's like asking, "on what page of Shakespeare's *Hamlet* do we find Shakespeare?" Shakespeare isn't confined to what he wrote—he's beyond it.

The God of the Bible created time and is not bound by it. When someone asks "who created God?" or "where did God come from?," these are action verbs that imply time is in existence prior to God. But nothing is prior to the God of the Bible!

So when someone asks, "where did God come from?" or "who created God?," technically, they're no longer referring to the God of the Bible but an alleged "created god." Here is a visual of that type of an alleged god:

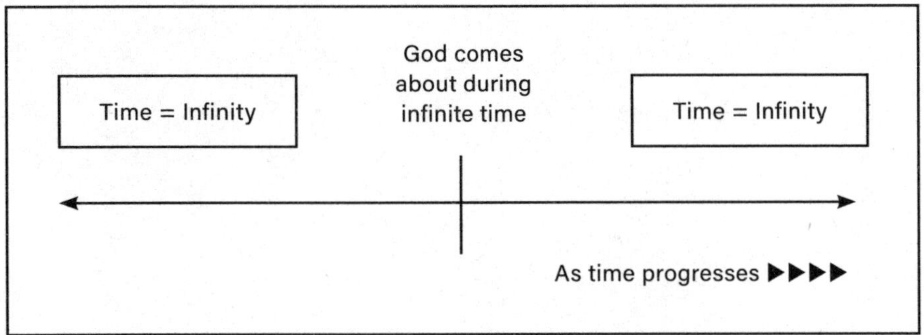

God is simply not bound by His creation but is beyond it so here's a visual of a more correct view of God:

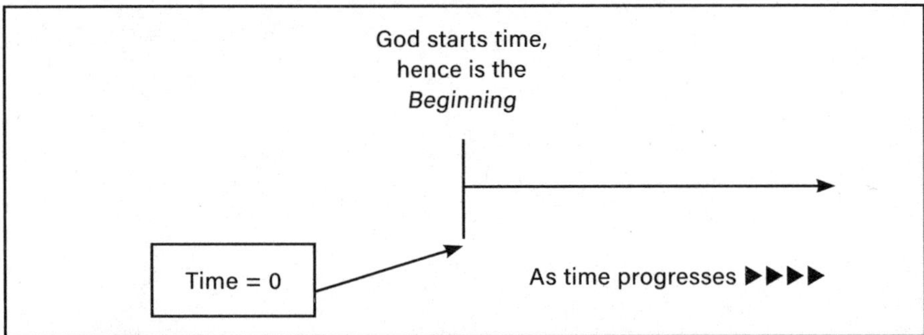

In Scripture, God is called the Ancient of Days, the Alpha and the Omega (first and last letters of the Greek alphabet), and the First and the Last because He is God over time.

- I watched till thrones were put in place, And the Ancient of Days was seated; His garment was white as snow, And the hair of His head was like pure wool. His throne was a fiery flame, Its wheels a burning fire. (Daniel 7:9)
- I am the Alpha and the Omega, the Beginning and the End, the First and the Last. (Revelation 22:13)

The God of the Bible created time and is not bound by it. God did not "show up" on a timeline at a given point. God is beyond time, is the God of time, and can see all time—past, present, and future. This is why God inspires prophecy with 100% accuracy.

Time is a constraint God created that is associated with created entities. God, however, is Lord over time.

God's Triune Nature

God is One.

In both the Old and New Testaments, the Bible is consistent about this truth regarding the nature of God (Deuteronomy 6:4[1]; Isaiah 44:8[2], 45:18[3]; Malachi 2:10[4]; Mark 12:29[5]; 1 Timothy 2:5[6]; James 2:19[7]). Yet, this one God is three persons of the one Godhead.

---

1. Hear, O Israel: The LORD our God, the LORD is one! (Deuteronomy 6:4)
2. "'Do not fear, nor be afraid; Have I not told you from that time, and declared it? You are My witnesses. Is there a God besides Me? Indeed there is no other Rock; I know not one.'" (Isaiah 44:8)
3. For thus says the LORD, Who created the heavens, Who is God, Who formed the earth and made it, Who has established it, Who did not create it in vain, Who formed it to be inhabited: "I *am* the LORD, and there is no other." (Isaiah 45:18)
4. Have we not all one Father? Has not one God created us? Why do we deal treacherously with one another By profaning the covenant of the fathers? (Malachi 2:10)
5. Jesus answered him, "The first of all the commandments is: 'Hear, O Israel, the LORD our God, the LORD is one." (Mark 12:29)
6. For there is one God and one Mediator between God and men, the Man Christ Jesus. (1 Timothy 2:5)
7. You believe that there is one God. You do well. Even the demons believe — and tremble! (James 2:19)

When defending the existence of God, you may also have to defend the nature of God, especially when witnessing to those trapped in cults, counterfeits of Christianity, or religions like Judaism or Islam. A knowledge of the biblical passages that support both the oneness and Triune nature of God is essential.

One God, Three Persons

There are numerous passages that teach that God the Father, God the Son, and God the Holy Spirit are distinct persons and yet each holds the attributes of deity. By taking all of Scripture into account, orthodox Christian theology has always affirmed that the one true God is Triune in nature—three co-equal and co-eternal persons in the Godhead (the doctrine of the Trinity).

The nature of our Triune God was first alluded to in the first chapter of the Bible, Genesis 1:26–27[8].

> "God said, 'Let us make man in our image.'"

Here "God" is a plural noun, "said" is in the third-person singular verb form, and we see both the plural pronoun "our" and the singular "His" referring to the same thing (God's image). This is not horribly confused grammar—it's God revealing His nature to us.

We are being introduced in Genesis, in a limited way, to the truth that God is a plurality in unity. We can't say from this verse that He is a trinity, but God progressively revealed more about Himself in later Scriptures to bring us to that conclusion. Even the first Hebrew name of God revealed to us in Genesis 1:1,[9] "Elohim," hints at His nature being a plural and yet used as a singular. We also read of His plural personhood and nature in the Tower of Babel account in Genesis 11:7[10] and also in Isaiah 6:8.[11]

---

8. Then God said, "Let Us make man in Our image, according to Our likeness; let them have dominion over the fish of the sea, over the birds of the air, and over the cattle, over all the earth and over every creeping thing that creeps on the earth." So God created man in His own image; in the image of God He created him; male and female He created them. (Genesis 1:26–27)
9. In the beginning God [Elohim אֱלוֹהַּ] created the heavens and the earth. (Genesis 1:1)
10. "Come, let Us go down and there confuse their language, that they may not understand one another's speech." (Genesis 11:7)
11. Also I heard the voice of the Lord, saying: "Whom shall I send, And who will go for Us?" Then I said, "Here *am* I! Send me." (Isaiah 6:8)

In Isaiah 48:12–16 the speaker in the passage describes Himself as the Creator and yet says that "the Lord God and His Spirit have sent Me." This is further hinting at the doctrine of the trinity, which becomes very clear in the New Testament. There are many other Old Testament Scriptures that hint at the same idea.

In Matthew 28:18–20[12], Jesus commands His disciples to baptize His followers in the name (singular) of the Father, Son, and Holy Spirit. John's gospel account tells us that "the Word" is God who became man in Jesus Christ (John 1:1–3[13], 1:14[14]). Jesus was fully man and fully God. Many other verses combine together to teach that God is Triune.

As a start on a thorough discussion on this topic, the following chart is an accumulation of many of the passages that show the deity of the Father, the Son, and the Holy Spirit.

The Bible Teaches: God Is Triune

	God, the Father...	God, the Son...	God, the Holy Spirit...
is the Creator	Genesis 1:1; 2:4; 14:19–22 Deuteronomy 32:6 Psalm 102:25 Isaiah 42:5; 45:18 Mark 13:19 1 Corinthians 8:6 Ephesians 3:9 Hebrews 2:10 Revelation 4:11	John 1:1-3 Colossians 1:16–17 1 Corinthians 8:6 Hebrew 1:2; 1:8–12	Genesis 1:2 Job 33:4 Psalm 104:30

12. And Jesus came and spoke to them, saying, "All authority has been given to Me in heaven and on earth. Go therefore and make disciples of all the nations, baptizing them in the name of the Father and of the Son and of the Holy Spirit, teaching them to observe all things that I have commanded you; and lo, I am with you always, even to the end of the age." Amen. (Matthew 28:18–20)
13. In the beginning was the Word, and the Word was with God, and the Word was God. He was in the beginning with God. All things were made through Him, and without Him nothing was made that was made. (John 1:1–3)
14. And the Word became flesh and dwelt among us, and we beheld His glory, the glory as of the only begotten of the Father, full of grace and truth. (John 1:14)

	God, the Father...	God, the Son...	God, the Holy Spirit...
is unchanging and eternal	Psalm 90:2 Psalm 102:25-27 Isaiah 43:10 Malachi 3:6	Micah 5:2 Colossians 1:17 Hebrews 1:8–12; 13:8 John 8:58	Hebrews 9:14
has a distinct will	Luke 22:42	Luke 22:42	Acts 13:2 1 Corinthians 12:11
accepts worship	Too many to list	Matthew 14:33 Hebrews 1:6	—
accepts prayer	Too many to list	John 14:14 Romans 10:9–13 2 Corinthians 12:8–9	—
is the Savior	Isaiah 43:11; 45:21 Hosea 13:4 1 Timothy 1:1	John 4:42 Acts 4:12; 13:23 Philippians 3:20 2 Timothy 1:10 Titus 1:4; 2:13; 3:6 2 Peter 1:11; 2:20; 3:18 1 John 4:14	John 3:5 1 Corinthians 12:3
is the mediator between God and man	N/A	1 Timothy 2:5 1 John 2:1	John 14:16; 14:26 Romans 8:26-27 Ephesians 2:18
has the power to resurrect	1 Thessalonians 1:8-10	John 2:19; 10:17	Romans 8:11
is called God	John 1:18; 6:27 Philippians 1:2; 2:11 Ephesians 4:6 2 Thessalonians 1:2	John 1:1-5; 1:14; 1:18; 20:28 Colossians 2:9 Hebrews 1:8 Titus 2:13	Acts 5:3-4 2 Corinthians 3:15-17

	God, the Father...	God, the Son...	God, the Holy Spirit...
is called *Mighty God*	Isaiah 10:21 Luke 22:69	Isaiah 9:6	—
is omnipresent/ everywhere	1 Kings 8:27 Isaiah 40:12	Matthew 28:18–20	Psalm 139:7–10
is omnipotent/ has power and authority	2 Chronicles 20:6; 25:8 Job 12:13 Romans 1:20 1 Corinthians 6:14 Jude 1:25	John 3:31; 3:35; 14:6; 16:15 Philippians 2:9–11	1 Samuel 11:6 Luke 1:35
is all-knowing	Psalm 139:2 Isaiah 46:10 1 John 3:20 Acts 15:8	John 16:30; 21:17	1 Corinthians 2:10–11
has the fullness of God in them (not just "a part of God")	N/A	Colossians 2:9	—
gives life	Genesis 1:21; 1:24; 2:7 Psalm 49:15 John 3:16, 5:21 1 Timothy 6:13	John 5:21; 14:6; 20:31 Romans 5:21	2 Corinthians 3:6 Romans 8:11
is in agreement with the Father	N/A	John 3:34; 8:42; 10:36; 14:24; 15:10 Galatians 4:4 1 John 4:14	Isaiah 42:1 John 3:34; 14:26 Galatians 4:6 1 Thessalonians 4:8
is in agreement with the Son	Matthew 26:53 John 14:16	N/A	John 14:16–17; 15:26 Luke 3:16

	God, the Father...	God, the Son...	God, the Holy Spirit...
is in agreement with the Spirit	—	Mark 1:12 Matthew 4:1 Luke 4:1	N/A
loves	John 3:16 Romans 8:39 Ephesians 6:23 1 John 4:16	Mark 10:21 John 15:9 Ephesians 5:25; 6:23	Romans 15:30
has ownership of believers	Psalm 24:1 John 8:47	Romans 7:4; 8:9	—
is distinct	Matthew 3:16–17; 28:19 John 17:1	Matthew 3:16–17; 4:1; 28:19 John 17:1	1 Samuel 19:20 Matthew 3:16–17; 4:1; 28:19
is one with the other persons in the trinity	Deuteronomy 6:4 1 Corinthians 8:6	John 10:30; 14:20	1 Corinthians 12:3–11
is judge	Genesis 18:25 Psalm 7:11; 50:6; 94:1–2; 96:13; 98:9 John 8:50 Romans 2:16	John 5:24–27 Acts 17:31 2 Corinthians 5:10 2 Timothy 4:1	—
forgives sin	Micah 7:18	Luke 7:47–50	—
claimed divinity	Exodus 20:2	Matthew 26:63–64	—
is uncreated/First and the Last/Beginning and the End	Isaiah 44:6	Revelation 1:17–18; 22:13	—
lives in the believer	John 14:23 2 Corinthians 6:16 1 John 3:24	John 14:20–23 Galatians 2:20 Colossians 1:27	John 14:16–17 Romans 8:11 1 Peter 1:11
has the godly title "I Am"	Exodus 3:14	John 8:58	

	God, the Father...	God, the Son...	God, the Holy Spirit...
is personal/ fellowships	1 John 1:3	1 Corinthians 1:9 1 John 1:3	Acts 13:2 2 Corinthians 13:14 Ephesians 4:30 Philippians 2:1
makes believers holy/sanctifies	1 Thessalonians 5:23	Colossians 1:22	1 Peter 1:2
upholds	Deuteronomy 8:3 Matthew 4:4	Colossians 1:17	—
knows the future	Isaiah 46:10 Jeremiah 29:11	Matthew 24:1–51; 26:64 John 16:32; 18:4	1 Samuel 10:10; 19:20 Luke 1:67, 2 Peter 1:21
is called "Lord of lords"	Deuteronomy 10:17 Psalm 136:3	Revelation 17:14; 19:16	—

The "Omni's" of God

Who is God? In the last chapter we learned to defend the nature of our Triune God; He is three in one. Here we will explore more of His character, nature, and essence, specifically the "omni's" of God: He is *omniscient* (all-knowing), *omnipotent* (all-powerful), and *omnipresent* (all-present).

These three attributes belong to the God of the Bible *alone* which sets Him apart from all other alleged gods or creators invented by sinful man.

In Acts 17, when Paul was preaching to the Greeks at Mars Hill (the Areopagus), he defined God as the Creator, the one who gives life and breath to all creatures and who needs nothing from us, unlike their idols "made with hands." Really, in Paul's description of God, he's appealing to this trifecta of "omni's."

It caught the attention of everyone listening to his sermon because, compared to the various forms of Greek mythology, including Stoicism and Epicureanism (evolutionism), the God of the Bible was so far beyond any of their gods (my comments added in bold):

> *God, who made the world and everything in it* **(God is Creator**

> **and omnipotent)**, *since He is Lord of heaven and earth* **(God is omnipotent)**, *does not dwell in temples made with hands. Nor is He worshiped with men's hands, as though He needed anything, since He gives to all life, breath, and all things* **(God is omnipotent)**. *And He has made from one blood every nation of men to dwell on all the face of the earth, and has determined their preappointed times and the boundaries of their dwellings* **(God is omnipotent and omniscient)**, *so that they should seek the Lord, in the hope that they might grope for Him and find Him, though He is not far from each one of us* **(God is omnipresent)**; *for in Him we live and move and have our being* **(God is omnipresent)**, *as also some of your own poets have said, 'For we are also His offspring.'* (Acts 17:24–28)

Omniscience

Omni means "all" in Latin. The second part of omniscience, the word *science*, simply means *knowledge* in its classical definition. In Webster's 1828 dictionary, it says that the "science of God must be perfect," indicative of God's omniscience.

Sadly, modern dictionary definitions often leave this out. Today, science has many definitions, including the observable and repeatable scientific method. But another newer definition is actually a religious one—studying the *natural world* through a strictly *naturalistic lens*. In other words, the methods of scientific observations have been confused and conflated with the religion of naturalism.

But back to the point, omniscience simply means *all-knowing*. God is all-knowing, something Scripture teaches over and over again:

- *For if our heart condemns us, God is greater than our heart, and knows all things* (1 John 3:20).
- *He counts the number of the stars; He calls them all by name. Great is our Lord, and mighty in power; His understanding is infinite* (Psalm 147:4–5).
- *Do you know how the clouds are balanced, Those wondrous works of Him who is perfect in knowledge?* (Job 37:16).
- *But the very hairs of your head are all numbered* (Matthew 10:30).

- *Have you not known? Have you not heard? The everlasting God, the LORD, The Creator of the ends of the earth, Neither faints nor is weary. His understanding is unsearchable* (Isaiah 40:28).
- *Behold, the former things have come to pass, And new things I declare; Before they spring forth I tell you of them. Sing to the LORD a new song, And His praise from the ends of the earth, You who go down to the sea, and all that is in it, You coastlands and you inhabitants of them!* (Isaiah 42:9–10).
- *For the word of God is living and powerful, and sharper than any two-edged sword, piercing even to the division of soul and spirit, and of joints and marrow, and is a discerner of the thoughts and intents of the heart. And there is no creature hidden from His sight, but all things are naked and open to the eyes of Him to whom we must give account* (Hebrews 4:12–13).

Omnipotence

Now that you know that *omni* means "all," let's turn to omnipotent or omnipotence. Potent means "power" or "force," from the Latin word *potentia*. This is also where we get our modern words potential or potency from.

In science, we learn about potential energy—think of God as having the ultimate or all the potential energy in all matters! Although analogies are not perfect, this example give hints about the omnipotence of God: He is all powerful in all respects.

Now you may've heard this objection to God's omnipotence, "If God is all-powerful, and can He do all things, can God sin?" Of course, when someone asks this question, he shows that he doesn't realize that a God who cannot keep His own Word would *not* be an omnipotent God but merely a "potent" *false* god, like the Greek "gods" (i.e., we would no longer be talking about the God of the Bible).

An all-powerful God is One who states His sovereign will and accomplishes it—a God who cannot sin or lie (2 Corinthians 5:21[1]; Titus 1:2[2]; Hebrews 4:15[3], 6:18[4]). A less powerful "god" states his puny will and is too weak

1. For He made Him who knew no sin to be sin for us, that we might become the righteousness of God in Him. (2 Corinthians 5:21)
2. In hope of eternal life which God, who cannot lie, promised before time began. (Titus 1:2)
3. For we do not have a High Priest who cannot sympathize with our weaknesses, but was in all points tempted as we are, yet without sin. (Hebrews 4:15)
4. That by two immutable things, in which it is impossible for God to lie, we might have strong consolation, who have fled for refuge to lay hold of the hope set before us. (Hebrews 6:18)

to accomplish it (i.e., sin). So, a good response could be that "to be an all-powerful God requires God to be powerful enough to keep from sinning, unlike a *less-than-all-powerful* god who could fail by sinning."

The God of the Bible is all-powerful, an attribute attested throughout Scripture, including by the fact that He's called "the Almighty" 48 times in the Old Testament and 10 times in the New Testament (58 total)!

- *Who being the brightness of His glory and the express image of His person, and upholding all things by the word of His power, when He had by Himself purged our sins, sat down at the right hand of the Majesty on high* (Hebrews 1:3).
- *But Jesus looked at them and said to them, "With men this is impossible, but with God all things are possible"* (Matthew 19:26).
- *I know that You can do everything, And that no purpose of Yours can be withheld from You* (Job 42:2).
- *Nature of being the Creator of all things* (Genesis 1:1–2:3, Exodus 20:11, Exodus 31:17, Nehemiah 9:6, John 1:1–3, Colossians 1:16–17, Hebrews 1, Psalm 33:6).
- *For since the creation of the world His invisible attributes are clearly seen, being understood by the things that are made, even His eternal power and Godhead, so that they are without excuse* (Romans 1:20).
- *Ah, Lord GOD! Behold, You have made the heavens and the earth by Your great power and outstretched arm. There is nothing too hard for You* (Jeremiah 32:17).
- *(As it is written, "I have made you a father of many nations") in the presence of Him whom he believed—God, who gives life to the dead and calls those things which do not exist as though they did* (Romans 4:17).
- *Indeed before the day was, I am He; And there is no one who can deliver out of My hand; I work, and who will reverse it?* (Isaiah 43:13).
- *For He spoke, and it was done; He commanded, and it stood fast* (Psalm 33:9).
- *Whatever the LORD pleases He does, In heaven and in earth, In the seas and in all deep places* (Psalm 135:6).
- *As for the Almighty, we cannot find Him; He is excellent in power, In judgment and abundant justice; He does not oppress* (Job 37:23).

Omnipresence

The word "presence" can be defined as the state of being present/existing in a specific place or moment in time. We as individual human beings (creatures) can only ever exist at a particular place and time—we live in the present. However, that's not the case for our Creator God, who is ever-present in all time, since He created time and is the Lord over time.

Scripture uses terms like He is the *Alpha and Omega* (which is roughly equivalent to A-Z in our modern alphabet), the *Beginning and the End*, that *He is before all things*, the *Ancient of Days*, and so on. These phrases show that God's nature is greater than time. Or simply put, God is beyond time.

Once people understand God's omnipresence, it can help them answer basic questions like those we answered in Chapter 16, "Where did God come from?" or "Who created God?" As we learned previously, when someone asks these types of questions, he is presuming that time is absolute and that God had to show up at some "point" on that timeline. But that's backwards! Time is *not* greater than God.

Think about it: If time was greater than God, then *God would not be God!* Instead that "god" would just be some false, created deity, not the God of the Bible, who is beyond time and created time itself. God is the *uncreated* being that brought time into existence in the first place, which can be easily seen from the very first verse of the Bible, Genesis 1:1, "In the *beginning*, God..." (emphasis added).

The Westminster children's catechism states the omnipresence of God in a very simple way (Question 12): "Does God know all things? Yes; nothing can be hid from God." This fact that, indeed, nothing can be hidden from God, is clearly seen in Scripture:

- *The eyes of the LORD are in every place, Keeping watch on the evil and the good* (Proverbs 15:3).
- *But will God indeed dwell on the earth? Behold, heaven and the heaven of heavens cannot contain You. How much less this temple which I have built!* (1 Kings 8:27).
- *LORD, You have searched me and known me* (Psalm 139:1, plus the rest of the Psalm).
- *Can anyone hide himself in secret places, So I shall not see him? says the LORD; Do I not fill heaven and earth? says the LORD* (Jeremiah 23:24).

- *Remember the former things of old, For I am God, and there is no other; I am God, and there is none like Me, Declaring the end from the beginning, And from ancient times things that are not yet done, Saying, 'My counsel shall stand, And I will do all My pleasure'* (Isaiah 46:9–10).
- *For the word of God is living and powerful, and sharper than any two-edged sword, piercing even to the division of soul and spirit, and of joints and marrow, and is a discerner of the thoughts and intents of the heart. And there is no creature hidden from His sight, but all things are naked and open to the eyes of Him to whom we must give account* (Hebrews 4:12–13).
- *And He is before all things, and in Him all things consist* (Colossians 1:17).
- *For where two or three are gathered together in My name, I am there in the midst of them* (Matthew 18:20).
- *Thus says the LORD: "Heaven is My throne, And earth is My footstool. Where is the house that you will build Me? And where is the place of My rest?"* (Isaiah 66:1).
- *So that they should seek the Lord, in the hope that they might grope for Him and find Him, though He is not far from each one of us* (Acts 17:27).
- *For His eyes are on the ways of man, And He sees all his steps* (Job 34:21).

The Lesser-Known Omni's of God

Most Christians are familiar with the "trifecta of omni's" as they're often cited and have been discussed by theologians throughout Church history. But there are other "omni's" of God and while the words themselves may not be familiar to you, the attribute they describe should be, including:

- Omniveritas (*veritas* means truth; thus, Omniveritas means all-truth)
- Omnivita (*vita* means life; thus, Omnivita means all-life-giving/sustaining)
- Omnibenevolence (*benevolence* means loving and kindness; thus, Omnibenevolence means all-love/loving in an all-kind way)
- Omniperfectio (*perfectio* means perfection; thus, Omniperfectio means all-perfect)
- Omnibonitas (*bonitas* means goodness; thus, Omnibonita means all-goodness)

- Omnisanctitas (*sanctitas* means holiness; thus, Omnisanctitas means all-holiness)
- Omnisapientia (*sapientia* means wisdom; thus, Omnisapientia means all-wisdom)
- Omniiustitia (*iustitia* means justice; thus Omniiustitia means all-just/justice)

Omniveritas (All-Truthful)

God is the truth (John 14:6[5]) and in Him there is no falsehood (Titus 1:2[6]). God is the standard of truth and the definition of it. The existence of truth is predicated on the existence of the *God of truth* (Deuteronomy 32:4[7]; Psalm 31:5[8]; Isaiah 65:16[9]).

Omnivita (All-Life-Giving/Sustaining)

God is life (John 14:6[10]). He is the Creator of life (Genesis 1) and the Giver of life (1 Corinthians 15:45[11]). He can resurrect Himself (John 10:17–18[12]) and can resurrect us (John 5:24[13]), some to everlasting life and some to everlasting punishment (e.g., Matthew 25:31–46). He created both physical and spiritual living beings (e.g., angels, heavenly hosts, and even Satan in his original perfect state prior to his willful sin against God).

---

5. Jesus said to him, "I am the way, the truth, and the life. No one comes to the Father except through Me." (John 14:6)
6. Ibid. Ref. 2.
7. He is the Rock, His work is perfect; For all His ways are justice, A God of truth and without injustice; Righteous and upright is He. (Deuteronomy 32:4)
8. Into Your hand I commit my spirit; You have redeemed me, O LORD God of truth. (Psalm 31:5)
9. So that he who blesses himself in the earth Shall bless himself in the God of truth; And he who swears in the earth Shall swear by the God of truth; Because the former troubles are forgotten, And because they are hidden from My eyes. (Isaiah 65:16)
10. Ibid. Ref 5.
11. And so it is written, "The first man Adam became a living being." The last Adam became a life-giving spirit. (1 Corinthians 15:45)
12. "Therefore My Father loves Me, because I lay down My life that I may take it again. No one takes it from Me, but I lay it down of Myself. I have power to lay it down, and I have power to take it again. This command I have received from My Father." (John 10:17–18)
13. "Most assuredly, I say to you, he who hears My word and believes in Him who sent Me has everlasting life, and shall not come into judgment, but has passed from death into life." (John 5:24)

Omnibenevolence (All-Loving)

God is love (1 John 4:8[14]). He defines love (1 Corinthians 13), and He is the standard of steadfast love (e.g., Romans 8:38–39[15]). His love is unconditional, eternal, and personal for His children. And God showed His love for us in that while we were still sinners, Christ died for us (Romans 5:8[16]).

In His Triune nature, the three persons of God (Father, Son, and Spirit) have perfect love and unity shared among them from all eternity. We can love because we are made in the image of a loving God (Genesis 1:27[17]). Reciprocally, when we love God, then we are to obey His commandments (John 14:15[18], 14:23–24[19]).

Benevolence has taken on the meaning of *kindness* in today's vernacular. Nevertheless, God is both all-loving and all-kindness, being the standard of both (e.g., Titus 3:4).

Omniperfectio (All-Perfect)

God's way is perfect, and He is the standard of perfection (Psalm 18:30[20]; 2 Samuel 22:31[21]). God's will is perfect (Romans 12:2), and His Law is perfect (Psalm 19:7). *Every work of God is perfect.* Deuteronomy 32:4 says:

> *He is the Rock, His work is perfect; for all His ways are justice, a God of truth and without injustice; righteous and upright is He.*

Of course, we should expect every work of God to be perfect because *He is perfect.* For example, His work of original creation was perfect. After

14. He who does not love does not know God, for God is love. (1 John 4:8)
15. For I am persuaded that neither death nor life, nor angels nor principalities nor powers, nor things present nor things to come, nor height nor depth, nor any other created thing, shall be able to separate us from the love of God which is in Christ Jesus our Lord. (Romans 8:38–39)
16. But God demonstrates His own love toward us, in that while we were still sinners, Christ died for us. (Romans 5:8)
17. So God created man in His own image; in the image of God He created him; male and female He created them. (Genesis 1:27)
18. "If you love Me, keep My commandments." (John 14:15)
19. Jesus answered and said to him, "If anyone loves Me, he will keep My word; and My Father will love him, and We will come to him and make Our home with him. He who does not love Me does not keep My words; and the word which you hear is not Mine but the Father's who sent Me." (John 14:23–24)
20. As for God, His way is perfect; The word of the LORD is proven; He is a shield to all who trust in Him. (Psalm 18:30)
21. From the brightness before Him Coals of fire were kindled (2 Samuel 22:31)

creating the universe in six days, God stated that everything He had made was "very good" (Genesis 1:31[22]). However, the Fall into sin in Genesis 3 ruined God's perfect creation.

This is why we need a *perfect Savior* (Christ) to save us from sin and death. And it's why we need a new heavens and new earth where creation will be restored to perfection with no sin, death, or suffering. God's perfect work through His perfect life, death, and Resurrection, accomplished salvation for believers. Thus, Christians get to spend eternity with our perfect God, in a new perfect creation, with new perfect bodies forever, enjoying God's perfect goodness forever. And all this is predicated on God's omniperfectus.

Omnibonitas (All-Good)

A rich young ruler, who was wondering what he could "do" to inherit eternal life, addressed Jesus with "good teacher," and Jesus' response revealed the nature of His Godhood:

> *So Jesus said to him, "Why do you call Me good? No one is good but One, that is, God."* (Luke 18:19)

Note that Jesus did not correct the young man for this belief. Rather, Jesus corrected this man's *view* of "goodness" (only God is good). So, Jesus is *not* denying His own goodness, instead He's questioning the man's definition of goodness and his view of God. Being God in the flesh, *Jesus is good*—He is the very standard of it as God is good (e.g., Psalm 143:10[23]). During Creation Week, God called things He had created "good" and at the culmination declared all things "very good." Again, God's works are perfect (as we saw in the previous section) and so His works are good—because of God's perfect goodness.

From the opposite perspective, we can see that God is good because He has no deceit and commits no sin (2 Corinthians 5:21[24]; 1 Peter 2:22[25]; 1 John 3:5[26]).

---

22. Then God saw everything that He had made, and indeed it was very good. So the evening and the morning were the sixth day. (Genesis 1:31)
23. Teach me to do Your will, For You are my God; Your Spirit is good. Lead me in the land of uprightness. (Psalm 143:10)
24. For He made Him who knew no sin to be sin for us, that we might become the righteousness of God in Him. (2 Corinthians 5:21)
25. Who committed no sin, Nor was deceit found in His mouth. (1 Peter 2:22)
26. And you know that He was manifested to take away our sins, and in Him there is no sin. (1 John 3:5)

Omnisanctitas (All-Holy)

In both the Old and New Testament, God is proclaimed as "Holy, holy, holy."

- *And one cried to another and said: "Holy, holy, holy is the LORD of hosts; The whole earth is full of His glory!"* (Isaiah 6:3).
- *The four living creatures, each having six wings, were full of eyes around and within. And they do not rest day or night, saying: "Holy, holy, holy, Lord God Almighty, Who was and is and is to come!"* (Revelation 4:8).

Holy means to be sacred and pure, and God is the very standard and source of sacredness and purity, even His name is holy (e.g., Psalm 103:1[27]; Ezekiel 39:7[28]). He is the thrice Holy God, and we are to emulate Him and be holy as well (1 Peter 1:15–16[29]).

Omnisapientia (All-Wise)

God is the source of all wisdom, and the perfection of wisdom is found only in Him. He gives wisdom to the wise and to those who fear Him. Even Solomon's wisdom for governing the nation of Israel was given by God (1 Kings 4:29[30]; 2 Chronicles 1:11–12[31]), and He bestowed on Daniel wisdom (Daniel 2:23[32]). God gives wisdom liberally and without reproach (Proverbs 2:6[33]; Ecclesiastes 2:26[34]; James 1:5[35]).

---

27. Bless the LORD, O my soul; And all that is within me, bless His holy name! (Psalm 103:1)
28. So I will make My holy name known in the midst of My people Israel, and I will not let them profane My holy name anymore. Then the nations shall know that I am the LORD, the Holy One in Israel. (Ezekiel 39:7)
29. But as He who called you is holy, you also be holy in all your conduct, because it is written, "Be holy, for I am holy." (1 Peter 1:15–16)
30. And God gave Solomon wisdom and exceedingly great understanding, and largeness of heart like the sand on the seashore. (1 Kings 4:29)
31. And God said to Solomon: "Because this was in your heart, and you have not asked riches or wealth or honor or the life of your enemies, nor have you asked long life — but have asked wisdom and knowledge for yourself, that you may judge My people over whom I have made you king — wisdom and knowledge are granted to you; and I will give you riches and wealth and honor, such as none of the kings have had who were before you, nor shall any after you have the like." (2 Chronicles 1:11–12)
32. "I thank You and praise You, O God of my fathers; You have given me wisdom and might, And have now made known to me what we asked of You, For You have made known to us the king's demand." (Daniel 2:23)
33. For the LORD gives wisdom; From His mouth come knowledge and understanding. (Proverbs 2:6)
34. For God gives wisdom and knowledge and joy to a man who is good in His sight; but to the sinner He gives the work of gathering and collecting, that he may give to him who is good before God. This also is vanity and grasping for the wind. (Ecclesiastes 2:26)
35. If any of you lacks wisdom, let him ask of God, who gives to all liberally and without reproach, and it will be given to him. (James 1:5)

Note that there is a distinction between sound or godly wisdom, which is from God (Proverbs 3:21[36]; James 3:17[37]), and counterfeit wisdom of the world (e.g., 1 Corinthians 3:19–20[38]; Colossians 2:23[39]; James 3:15–16[40]). There is no legitimate human (worldly) wisdom or understanding that can stand against the Lord and His perfect and infinite wisdom (Proverbs 21:30[41]).

In our human state, the fear of the Lord is the beginning of wisdom (Proverbs 9:10[42]). And as mankind, we can grow and learn in understanding and wisdom. When Jesus took on flesh and became a man, He emptied Himself of His infinite godly wisdom and became the babe in the manger (Philippians 2:1–11). He too had to grow in wisdom:

- *And the Child grew and became strong in spirit, filled with wisdom; and the grace of God was upon Him* (Luke 2:40).
- *And Jesus increased in wisdom and stature, and in favor with God and men* (Luke 2:52).

And upon His Resurrection, all authority had returned to Him (past tense) (e.g., Matthew 28:18[43]; Jude 1:25[44]), and, being fully God and fully man, He has all the treasures of wisdom and knowledge hidden in Him (Colossians 2:3[45]).

36. My son, let them not depart from your eyes — Keep sound wisdom and discretion. (Proverbs 3:21)
37. But the wisdom that is from above is first pure, then peaceable, gentle, willing to yield, full of mercy and good fruits, without partiality and without hypocrisy. (James 3:17)
38. For the wisdom of this world is foolishness with God. For it is written, "He catches the wise in their own craftiness"; and again, "The LORD knows the thoughts of the wise, that they are futile." (1 Corinthians 3:19–20)
39. These things indeed have an appearance of wisdom in self-imposed religion, false humility, and neglect of the body, but are of no value against the indulgence of the flesh. (Colossians 2:23)
40. This wisdom does not descend from above, but is earthly, sensual, demonic. For where envy and self-seeking exist, confusion and every evil thing are there. (James 3:15–16)
41. There is no wisdom or understanding or counsel against the LORD. (Proverbs 21:30)
42. The fear of the LORD is the beginning of wisdom, And the knowledge of the Holy One is understanding. (Proverbs 9:10)
43. And Jesus came and spoke to them, saying, "All authority has been given to Me in heaven and on earth." (Matthew 28:18)
44. To God our Savior, Who alone is wise, Be glory and majesty, Dominion and power, Both now and forever. Amen. (Jude 1:25)
45. In whom are hidden all the treasures of wisdom and knowledge. (Colossians 2:3)

Omniiustitia (All-Just/Justice)

God is a *just* God and the *righteous* Judge of all (Isaiah 45:21[46]; Psalm 75:7[47]; Ecclesiastes 3:17[48]; Hebrews 12:23[49]; 2 Timothy 4:8[50]). This is why God judges *all* sin (from the first sins of Satan, Adam, and Eve [in Genesis 3] to the final judgment):

- *He who rejects Me, and does not receive My words, has that which judges him – the word that I have spoken will judge him in the last day* (John 12:48).

God is the perfect standard of being just, and His justice is absolute and without flaw for God shows no partiality and takes no bribe (e.g.,Deuteronomy 10:17[51]; Proverbs 20:23[52]; Romans 2:11[53]). This is why even for just *one* sin against a perfect and Holy God we deserve an infinite and just punishment (James 2:10[54]). Yet God in His infinite wisdom took the punishment on behalf of guilty sinners. The infinite Son of God, Jesus Christ, took that punishment, and the wrath of God was poured out on Him (Isaiah 53:10-11[55]; 1 Corinthians 15:3-4[56]; 1 Peter 2:24[57])

---

46. Tell and bring forth your case; Yes, let them take counsel together. Who has declared this from ancient time? Who has told it from that time? Have not I, the LORD? And there is no other God besides Me, A just God and a Savior; There is none besides Me. (Isaiah 45:21)
47. But God is the Judge: He puts down one, And exalts another. (Psalm 75:7)
48. I said in my heart, "God shall judge the righteous and the wicked, For there is a time there for every purpose and for every work." (Ecclesiastes 3:17)
49. To the general assembly and church of the firstborn who are registered in heaven, to God the Judge of all, to the spirits of just men made perfect. (Hebrews 12:23)
50. Finally, there is laid up for me the crown of righteousness, which the Lord, the righteous Judge, will give to me on that Day, and not to me only but also to all who have loved His appearing. (2 Timothy 4:8)
51. "For the LORD your God is God of gods and Lord of lords, the great God, mighty and awesome, who shows no partiality nor takes a bribe." (Deuteronomy 10:17)
52. Diverse weights are an abomination to the LORD, And dishonest scales are not good. (Proverbs 20:23)
53. For there is no partiality with God. (Romans 2:11)
54. For whoever shall keep the whole law, and yet stumble in one point, he is guilty of all. (James 2:10)
55. Yet it pleased the LORD to bruise Him; He has put Him to grief. When You make His soul an offering for sin, He shall see His seed, He shall prolong His days, And the pleasure of the LORD shall prosper in His hand. He shall see the labor of His soul, and be satisfied. By His knowledge My righteous Servant shall justify many, For He shall bear their iniquities. (Isaiah 53:10–11)
56. For I delivered to you first of all that which I also received: that Christ died for our sins according to the Scriptures, and that He was buried, and that He rose again the third day according to the Scriptures. (1 Corinthians 15:3–4)
57. Who Himself bore our sins in His own body on the tree, that we, having died to sins, might live for righteousness — by whose stripes you were healed. (1 Peter 2:24)

Concluding the Omni's

Of course, there are other omni's of God that I could have listed, but these ones should be sufficient to show that God is the standard. Again, there is no standard greater than God for all matters. He is the ultimate source and highest basis for all things like knowledge, power, existence, life, wisdom, goodness, and so on.

We often think of the trifecta of omni's, but Christ has lordship over all things—in heaven *and* on earth (e.g., Psalm 2:8[58], 103:19[59]; Matthew 6:10[60], 28:18[61]). Or in the words of Abraham Kuyper,

> There is not a square inch in the whole domain of our human existence over which Christ, who is Sovereign over all, does not cry, Mine![62]

58. Ask of Me, and I will give You The nations for Your inheritance, And the ends of the earth for Your possession. (Psalm 2:8)
59. The LORD has established His throne in heaven, And His kingdom rules over all. (Psalm 103:19)
60. Your kingdom come. Your will be done On earth as it is in heaven. (Matthew 6:10)
61. Ibid. Ref. 43.
62. Abraham Kuyper, *Sphere Sovereignty*, as referenced in Roger Henderson, Kuyper's Inch, Pro Rege, Volume 36, Number 3, 2008, pp. 12-14, https://digitalcollections.dordt.edu/cgi/viewcontent.cgi?article=1380&context=prorege#lf.

The Distressing Attributes of God

"You say God is a God of love? Well, what about this verse…?"

Have you ever been witnessing to someone, sharing with them the goodness of God, only to have them sneeringly bring up Scriptures about God's hate or His jealousy, wrath, anger, or vengeance, asking you to explain that?

Many Christians freeze having only focused on the "nice" attributes of God: His grace, kindness, mercy, patience, and especially love.

God's other attributes, like His perfect justice, righteous anger, righteous hate, righteous jealousy, righteous wrath, and righteous vengeance are often overlooked—but they are just as much attributes of who God is as His other attributes. The only reason we find them uncomfortable or even distressing is because when we don't understand the righteous forms of anger, hate, or jealousy, and confuse them with the unrighteous forms of anger, hate, or jealousy that we as human often exhibit.

This confusion affects how we view the nature and character of God, and makes it easy to fall into the trap of mistaken views of anger, hate, jealousy, wrath, and vengeance. For example, it's popular among Christians to believe that hate is a sin. Yet God is often describing as hating various sins and even individuals. Obviously God cannot sin (Hebrews 4:15[1]; 1 John 1:5[2]; 2 Corinthians 5:21[3]; Deuteronomy 32:4[4]), therefore it's clearly our view of hate that is wrong.

Or what about jealousy? We've all been taught that's a sin and yet the Ten Commandments reads:

> *You shall not bow down to them nor serve them.* ***For I, the Lord your God, am a jealous God,*** *visiting the iniquity of the fathers on the children to the third and fourth generations of those who hate Me.* (Exodus 20:5, emphasis added)

God (and by extension His Word) is the absolute authority in all matters, including in describing His own attributes. When our perception of reality is refuted by God's Word, it's our perception, not God's Word, that needs to change. As fallible, sinful beings (Romans 3:23[5], 5:12[6]), our perceptions and thoughts can be wrong. To correct them, we need to align our views with God's Word.

When we do that, we start to think properly (i.e., think God's thoughts after Him) and develop a fuller picture of who our Creator God actually is, not the version our culture or modern Christianity has constructed.

Anger

This may surprise you, but one of God's righteous attributes is *anger*. Consider the time God spoke through Moses to the Israelites, predicting that they would provoke God to anger after Moses dies (Deuteronomy 31:29[7]):

1. For we do not have a High Priest who cannot sympathize with our weaknesses, but was in all points tempted as we are, yet without sin. (Hebrews 4:15)
2. This is the message which we have heard from Him and declare to you, that God is light and in Him is no darkness at all. (1 John 1:5)
3. For He made Him who knew no sin to be sin for us, that we might become the righteousness of God in Him. (2 Corinthians 5:21)
4. He is the Rock, His work is perfect; For all His ways are justice, A God of truth and without injustice; Righteous and upright is He. (Deuteronomy 32:4)
5. For all have sinned and fall short of the glory of God. (Romans 3:23)
6. Therefore, just as through one man sin entered the world, and death through sin, and thus death spread to all men, because all sinned. (Romans 5:12)
7. For I know that after my death you will become utterly corrupt, and turn aside from the way which I have commanded you; and evil will befall you in the latter days, because you will do evil in the sight of the LORD, to provoke Him to anger through the work of your hands. (Deuteronomy 31:29)

They provoked Him to jealousy with foreign gods; with abominations they provoked Him to anger. (Deuteronomy 32:16)

Here, the prediction is that the Israelites would serve false gods and perform abominations that would make God angry. And, yes, if you know your Bible, you know the Israelites did indeed provoke God to anger many times (e.g., Judges 2:12[8]; 1 Kings 22:53[9]; 2 Chronicles 28:25[10]; Isaiah 1:4[11]).

What about the New Testament? Although the Bible doesn't use the term "*anger*," it seems appropriate to say Jesus was angry when He drove out the thieving money changers with a whip and overturned their tables in the temple (e.g., Matthew 21:12–13[12]; Mark 11:15[13]; John 2:15[14]).

God has perfect righteousness, so His anger is righteous anger and God cannot sin in His anger.

Man, being made in the image of God, can also have righteous anger. But as sinful human beings, we need to be careful not to sin in that anger—and it's more likely that we will sin in our anger! Consider that James contrasts man's anger (which is a quick anger) with God's by saying our anger doesn't bring about the righteousness that God desires[15] and Ephesians tells us not to sin in our anger.[16] Man's unrighteous anger, which we're all familiar with, is why people have a negative view of anger.

---

8. And they forsook the LORD God of their fathers, who had brought them out of the land of Egypt; and they followed other gods from among the gods of the people who were all around them, and they bowed down to them; and they provoked the LORD to anger. (Judges 2:12)
9. For he served Baal and worshiped him, and provoked the LORD God of Israel to anger, according to all that his father had done. (1 Kings 22:53)
10. And in every single city of Judah he made high places to burn incense to other gods, and provoked to anger the LORD God of his fathers. (2 Chronicles 28:25)
11. Alas, sinful nation, A people laden with iniquity, A brood of evildoers, Children who are corrupters! They have forsaken the LORD, They have provoked to anger The Holy One of Israel, They have turned away backward. (Isaiah 1:4)
12. Then Jesus went into the temple of God and drove out all those who bought and sold in the temple, and overturned the tables of the money changers and the seats of those who sold doves. And He said to them, "It is written, 'My house shall be called a house of prayer,' but you have made it a 'den of thieves.'" (Matthew 21:12–13)
13. So they came to Jerusalem. Then Jesus went into the temple and began to drive out those who bought and sold in the temple, and overturned the tables of the money changers and the seats of those who sold doves. (Mark 11:15)
14. When He had made a whip of cords, He drove them all out of the temple, with the sheep and the oxen, and poured out the changers' money and overturned the tables. (John 2:15)
15. Know this, my beloved brothers: let every person be quick to hear, slow to speak, slow to anger; for the anger of man does not produce the righteousness of God. (James 1:19–20, ESV)
16. Be angry and do not sin; do not let the sun go down on your anger. (Ephesians 4:26)

Unrighteous anger is why we're told not to make friends with an angry man, let we become ensnared in his ways,[17] and why sin is said to be crouching at the door of an angry person. Consider Cain, who did not sacrifice the same way that God did in Genesis 3:21[18] (a blood sacrifice for sin), but only offered first fruits. God didn't respect that offering, whereas God accepted Abel's blood sacrifice. This made Cain very angry (Genesis 4:5–6[19]). Cain *should* have been angry *with himself* for not making a pleasing sacrifice, and this anger should have helped him realize that he needed to make the correct sacrifice so that his offering would be accepted.

But Cain, in an unrighteous manner, directed his anger toward his brother. God warned him that sin was at his door (Genesis 4:7[20]), but he didn't rein in his anger. Instead, Cain succumbed to sinning in that anger when he killed his brother Abel.

Contrast this case of anger with that of Moses who mimicked the righteous anger of God when he saw sin in the Israelite camp. Here's the context: in Numbers chapters 26–31 Midianite women were seducing the Israelite men at Peor to sin against God and serve false gods like Baal. After a plague, God sent the Israelites to war to wipe out the Midianites involved in this seduction. But the Israelite army kept the very women alive who instigated the seduction—and the soldiers wanted to bring the women into their houses as personal captives and part of the plunder! This seduction and deception by pagan women had been a massive warning from God, and they ignored it. Moses was angered because they didn't follow God's instructions:

> *But Moses was angry with the officers of the army, with the captains over thousands and captains over hundreds, who had come from the battle. And Moses said to them: "Have you kept all the women alive? Look, these women caused the children of Israel, through the counsel of Balaam, to trespass against the Lord in the incident of Peor, and there was a plague among the congregation of the Lord. Now therefore, kill every male*

17. Make no friendship with a man given to anger, nor go with a wrathful man, lest you learn his ways and entangle yourself in a snare. (Proverbs 22:24–25)
18. And the LORD God made for Adam and for his wife garments of skins and clothed them. (Genesis 3:21, ESV)
19. But He did not respect Cain and his offering. And Cain was very angry, and his countenance fell. So the LORD said to Cain, "Why are you angry? And why has your countenance fallen?" (Genesis 4:5–6)
20. "If you do well, will you not be accepted? And if you do not do well, sin lies at the door. And its desire is for you, but you should rule over it." (Genesis 4:7)

among the little ones, and kill every woman who has known a man intimately. But keep alive for yourselves all the young girls who have not known a man intimately. (Numbers 31:14–18)

In his anger, Moses' actions endeavored to follow what God said and was meant to push the Israelites back on track with God's commands. In both cases, Cain and Moses were angry, and as a result people died. In Cain's case, it opposed God's Word; in Moses' case, it was in accordance with God's Word.[21]

The point is that anger is not always a sin, but in many cases it is a sin and the actions that flow from that anger only compound the sin. Anger that goes against God's Word is always unrighteous and sinful anger. And that is not the anger of God; His is a slow anger that burns against sin and those who refuse to repent of it. His righteous anger is always in step with His perfect justice and His perfect love.

Hate

Like His anger, Scripture also speaks of God's hatred, particularly towards sin but also towards sinners (e.g. Psalm 11:5[22], Psalm 5:5,[23] Hosea 9:15[24]). A perfectly righteous God (Romans 9:14[25]) can hate with perfectly justified hatred (i.e., without malice). Therefore God can both "love the world" (John 3:16), "have no pleasure in the death of the wicked" (Ezekiel 33:11), and want "all to reach repentance" (2 Peter 3:9), while still proclaiming "his [God's] soul hates the wicked and the one who loves violence" (Psalm 11:5).

The Bible says there is a time for hate.[26] Hate is even something God *commands* of us:

---

21. This example raises the question "how could God (or Moses) command the death of women and children during the Conquest?" Find answers to that objection in "Slaughter at Jericho," found at AnswersinGenesis.org. https://answersingenesis.org/contradictions-in-the-bible/slaughter-at-jericho/
22. The Lord tests the righteous, but his soul hates the wicked and the one who loves violence. (Psalm 11:5, ESV)
23. The boastful shall not stand before your eyes; you hate all evildoers. (Psalm 5:5)
24. Every evil of theirs is in Gilgal; there I began to hate them. Because of the wickedness of their deeds I will drive them out of my house. I will love them no more; all their princes are rebels. (Hosea 9:15)
25. What shall we say then? Is there unrighteousness with God? Certainly not! (Romans 9:14)
26. A time to love, and a time to hate; a time of war, and a time of peace. (Ecclesiastes 3:8)

> *You who love the Lord, hate evil! He preserves the souls of His saints; He delivers them out of the hand of the wicked.* (Psalm 97:10)

> *The fear of the Lord is to hate evil; pride and arrogance and the evil way and the perverse mouth I hate.* (Proverbs 8:13)

> *Hate evil, love good; establish justice in the gate. It may be that the Lord God of hosts will be gracious to the remnant of Joseph.* (Amos 5:15)

We are commanded to hate specific forms of evil that we may reflect God's righteous hatred for these very things. In poetic language, the book of Proverbs points out six things that God hates, and seven that are an abomination:

> *These six things the Lord hates, yes, seven are an abomination to Him: a proud look, a lying tongue, hands that shed innocent blood, a heart that devises wicked plans, feet that are swift in running to evil, a false witness who speaks lies, and one who sows discord among brethren.* (Proverbs 6:16–19)

Throughout Scripture, the six things God hates to go along with these seven abominations are:

1. Pride (Proverbs 8:13[27])
2. Arrogance (Proverbs 8:13[28])
3. The evil way (Proverbs 8:13[29])
4. The perverse mouth (Proverbs 8:13[30])
5. False worship (Deuteronomy 12:30–31[31], 16:21–22[32])

27. The fear of the LORD *is* to hate evil; Pride and arrogance and the evil way And the perverse mouth I hate. (Proverbs 8:13)
28. Ibid.
29. Ibid.
30. Ibid.
31. "Take heed to yourself that you are not ensnared to follow them, after they are destroyed from before you, and that you do not inquire after their gods, saying, 'How did these nations serve their gods? I also will do likewise.' You shall not worship the LORD your God in that way; for every abomination to the LORD which He hates they have done to their gods; for they burn even their sons and daughters in the fire to their gods." (Deuteronomy 12:30–31)
32. "You shall not plant for yourself any tree, as a wooden image, near the altar which you build for yourself to the LORD your God. You shall not set up a sacred pillar, which the LORD your God hates." (Deuteronomy 16:21–22)

6. The love of violence (Psalm 11:5[33])

In the Bible, we see reflections of God's hatred for lying, arrogance, evil ways, and violence:

> *I hate and abhor lying, but I love Your law.* (Psalm 119:163)
>
> *The boastful shall not stand in Your sight; You hate all workers of iniquity.* (Psalm 5:5)
>
> *Through Your precepts I get understanding; therefore I hate every false way.* (Psalm 119:104)
>
> *I hate the double-minded, but I love Your law.* (Psalm 119:113)
>
> *Therefore all Your precepts concerning all things I consider to be right; I hate every false way.* (Psalm 119:128)
>
> *Do I not hate them, O Lord, who hate You? And do I not loathe those who rise up against You?* (Psalm 139:21)
>
> *I hate them with perfect hatred; I count them my enemies.* (Psalm 139:22)
>
> *I hate, I despise your [false, hypocritical] feast days, and I do not savor your sacred assemblies.* (Amos 5:21)

Yes, we are called to hate and can righteously hate sin and those who willfully practice it. But we need to balance this with the whole counsel of God; hating evil, lying, pride, and so on is not in contradiction with the command of our Lord to love our enemies (Matthew 5:43–44[34]). As we saw earlier, God both hates the wicked and yet does not take pleasure in their death and sends good gifts (theologians call this "common grace") on both the wicked and the good (Matthew 5:45[35]). We are commanded to

33. The LORD tests the righteous, But the wicked and the one who loves violence His soul hates. (Psalm 11:5)
34. "You have heard that it was said, 'You shall love your neighbor and hate your enemy.' But I say to you, love your enemies, bless those who curse you, do good to those who hate you, and pray for those who spitefully use you and persecute you." (Matthew 5:43–44)
35. For he makes his sun rise on the evil and on the good, and sends rain on the just and on the unjust. (Matthew 5:45, ESV)

hate sin and evil but to have mercy for the sinner (e.g., Jude 1:22–23[36]). In mimicking God, we should develop the same hatred of sin that God has (i.e., not being afraid to point out sin but without hypocrisy), which is among the most loving things we can do for others. And the primary way we can show the same mercy we've received to other sinners is by pointing them to Christ and His sacrifice, which is the only way for their (and our) sins to be forgiven.

We also must remember that God can righteously hate sinners because God is omniscient, He knows their hearts and if they will ever repent. We, as fallible and sinful human beings, are not in God's all-knowing position—only God sees the end from the beginning. We are to hate sin, but at the same time love our enemies, praying God will use our obedience to bring people to repentance. This is part of the process of sanctification, becoming more pure and holy as the Holy Spirit conforms us to Christ's image (Romans 8:29[37]; 2 Thessalonians 2:13[38]).

Jealousy

As we read in the Ten Commandments, God is a jealous God (Exodus 20:5[39]). Furthermore, one of God's names is "Jealous."

> *For you shall worship no other god, for the Lord, whose name is Jealous, is a jealous God.* (Exodus 34:14)

Contextually, God is commanding the Israelites to destroy the idols and pagan places of worship in the land of Canaan; God warns that when they and their children follow the nations around them into pagan religious worship, they are no longer godly, but are instead considered adulterers playing the harlot:

---

36. And on some have compassion, making a distinction; but others save with fear, pulling them out of the fire, hating even the garment defiled by the flesh. (Jude 1:22–23)
37. For whom He foreknew, He also predestined to be conformed to the image of His Son, that He might be the firstborn among many brethren. (Romans 8:29)
38. But we are bound to give thanks to God always for you, brethren beloved by the Lord, because God from the beginning chose you for salvation through sanctification by the Spirit and belief in the truth. (2 Thessalonians 2:13)
39. You shall not bow down to them nor serve them. For I, the LORD your God, am a jealous God, visiting the iniquity of the fathers on the children to the third and fourth generations of those who hate Me. (Exodus 20:5)

But you shall destroy their altars, break their sacred pillars, and cut down their wooden images (for you shall worship no other god, for the Lord, whose name is Jealous, is a jealous God), lest you make a covenant with the inhabitants of the land, and they play the harlot with their gods and make sacrifice to their gods, and one of them invites you and you eat of his sacrifice, and you take of his daughters for your sons, and his daughters play the harlot with their gods and make your sons play the harlot with their gods. (Exodus 34:13–16)

God is consistent in the Bible about His jealousy when His people are unfaithful to Him. God is jealous for His name and for the worship of His people—He will not share His glory with another. His jealousy is like the jealousy of husband or a wife who wants their spouse to be faithful to them—they have every right to expect their spouse to remain faithful since they made a covenant with one another (though that kind of jealousy in humans can easily slide into sin—God's is always righteous).

God's jealousy is not the petty jealousy, grounded in envy and covetousness (James 3:14,[40] Exodus 20:17,[41] 1 Corinthians 3:3,[42] Romans 13:13[43]), that we as sinful humans often exhibit. That kind of jealousy is a sin and it's dangerous (Proverbs 6:34,[44] 27:4[45]). God's jealousy is righteous and leads him to justly pour out His wrath against sin,

"For in My jealousy and in the fire of My wrath I have spoken: 'Surely in that day there shall be a great earthquake in the land of Israel.'" (Ezekiel 38:19)

---

40. But if you have bitter jealousy and selfish ambition in your hearts, do not boast and be false to the truth. (James 3:14, ESV)
41. "You shall not covet your neighbor's house; you shall not covet your neighbor's wife, or his male servant, or his female servant, or his ox, or his donkey, or anything that is your neighbor's." (Exodus 20:17)
42. For while there is jealousy and strife among you, are you not of the flesh and behaving only in a human way? (1 Corinthians 3:3b, ESV)
43. Let us walk properly as in the daytime, not in orgies and drunkenness, not in sexual immorality and sensuality, not in quarreling and jealousy. (Romans 13:13, ESV)
44. For jealousy makes a man furious, and he will not spare when he takes revenge. (Proverbs 6:34, ESV)
45. Wrath is cruel, anger is overwhelming, but who can stand before jealousy? (Proverbs 27:4)

Wrath and Vengeance

God is a just God, and He enacts perfect justice on those who deserve it.

> *For we know Him who said, "Vengeance is Mine, I will repay," says the Lord. And again, "The Lord will judge His people." It is a fearful thing to fall into the hands of the living God.* (Hebrews 10:30–31)

Many times in the Bible, God Himself, or a man, men, or an angel, would enact His judgment, vengeance, and wrath. See the brief examples below:

Man/men: *"Take vengeance on the Midianites for the children of Israel. Afterward you shall be gathered to your people." So Moses spoke to the people, saying, "Arm some of yourselves for war, and let them go against the Midianites to take vengeance for the Lord on Midian."* (Numbers 31:2–3)

Angel: *And God sent an angel to Jerusalem to destroy it. As he was destroying, the Lord looked and relented of the disaster, and said to the angel who was destroying, "It is enough; now restrain your hand." And the angel of the Lord stood by the threshing floor of Ornan the Jebusite.* (1 Chronicles 21:15)

God: *And God said to Noah, "The end of all flesh has come before Me, for the earth is filled with violence through them; and behold, I will destroy them with the earth."* (Genesis 6:13)

God, being provoked to wrath by sin, shows that wrath is not a sin. Rather it is His just reaction, because of His perfect, holy nature, to sin. God's wrath—His determined, set opposition to sin—is a solemn, sobering reminder of the awfulness of sin and just how repugnant it is to God. We may not take it seriously; God always does. And God, being a righteous judge (2 Timothy 4:8[46]), must punish sin—and He does:

> *Also at Taberah and Massah and Kibroth Hattaavah you provoked the Lord to wrath.* (Deuteronomy 9:22)

> *Nevertheless the Lord did not turn from the fierceness of His great wrath, with which His anger was aroused against Judah, because of all the provocations with which Manasseh had provoked Him.* (2 Kings 23:26)

46. Finally, there is laid up for me the crown of righteousness, which the Lord, the righteous Judge, will give to me on that Day, and not to me only but also to all who have loved His appearing. (2 Timothy 4:8)

> *But because our fathers provoked the God of heaven to wrath, He gave them into the hand of Nebuchadnezzar king of Babylon, the Chaldean, who destroyed this temple and carried the people away to Babylon.* (Ezra 5:12)

> *"For thus says the Lord of hosts: 'Just as I determined to punish you When your fathers provoked Me to wrath,' Says the Lord of hosts, 'And I would not relent.'"* (Zechariah 8:14)

> *Now out of His mouth goes a sharp sword, that with it He should strike the nations. And He Himself will rule them with a rod of iron. He Himself treads the winepress of the fierceness and wrath of Almighty God.* (Revelation 19:15)

Ultimately God's wrath against sin is most plainly see in the Cross, when God poured out His wrath on His very Son[47] who bore our sins on His own body[48] (having none of His own sin to die for[49]). In dying in our place, Jesus drank the cup of God's wrath dry for us who believe. There is now no condemnation (no wrath) for those in Christ.[50] But for those still outside Christ, Jesus is coming again (that's a promise from God) and He will "tread the winepress of the fierceness and wrath of Almighty God" (Revelation 19:15) against the sins of those who refuse to repent. If you have never come to Christ, come to Him today!

Wrath and vengeance are not sins, though we are told to let God enact such things (Romans 12:19[51]). God, in His perfect wisdom, knowledge, and power, can and will do this justly, in the perfect time, and in right proportion to the sin. For those who are unrepentant, this should be a fearful thing.

---

47. Since, therefore, we have now been justified by his blood, much more shall we be saved by him from the wrath of God. (Romans 5:9, ESV)
48. He himself bore our sins in his body on the tree, that we might die to sin and live to righteousness. (1 Peter 2:24a, ESV)
49. For our sake he made him to be sin who knew no sin, so that in him we might become the righteousness of God. (2 Corinthians 5:21, ESV)
50. There is therefore now no condemnation to those who are in Christ Jesus, who do not walk according to the flesh, but according to the Spirit. (Romans 8:1)
51. Beloved, do not avenge yourselves, but rather give place to wrath; for it is written, "Vengeance is Mine, I will repay," says the Lord. (Romans 12:19)

Where Do You Stand?

Sinners may wish the wrath of God on Earth were temporal in nature but God is an eternal God, and we are made in God's eternal image. Your soul—every soul—*will* go on forever.

If you have not repented and turned to Jesus Christ in faith, who bore the wrath of our sin upon Himself (Isaiah 53), God's wrath should cause you to wake up and think about your eternity. God, being a righteous Judge, will judge sin with eternal consequences and you, like everyone else, have sinned and have no righteousness of your own (Romans 3:23).

And don't think you will escape by assuming, as many wrongly do, that the so-called "God of the Old Testament" is different from the supposedly non-wrathful God of the New Testament. The God of the Old Testament is the same consistent God in the New Testament (e.g., Malachi 3:6[52]; Hebrews 13:8[53]).

> *And many of those who sleep in the dust of the earth shall awake, Some to everlasting life, Some to shame and everlasting contempt.* (Daniel 12:2)

> *And these will go away into everlasting punishment, but the righteous into eternal life.* (Matthew 25:46)

When it comes down to it, it really is a fearful thing to fall into the hands of God.

> *And do not fear those who kill the body but cannot kill the soul. But rather fear Him who is able to destroy both soul and body in hell.* (Matthew 10:28)

And this is what hell is: hell is eternal, conscious punishment with the wrath of God on unrepentant sinners for all eternity.

> *He who believes in the Son has everlasting life; and he who does not believe the Son shall not see life, but the wrath of God abides on him.* (John 3:36)

---

52. "For I am the LORD, I do not change; Therefore you are not consumed, O sons of Jacob." (Malachi 3:6)
53. Jesus Christ is the same yesterday, today, and forever. (Hebrews 13:8)

But Jesus Christ, the eternal and infinitely powerful Son of God, took the wrath of sin upon Himself (Hebrews 9:26[54]) and made salvation possible by His death, burial, and Resurrection (Romans 10:9[55]). It's amazing to know our loving God did something for us in that while we were still sinners, Christ died for us (Romans 5:8[56]).

> *The Lord is not slack concerning His promise, as some count slackness, but is longsuffering toward us, not willing that any should perish but that all should come to repentance.* (2 Peter 3:9)

---

54. He then would have had to suffer often since the foundation of the world; but now, once at the end of the ages, He has appeared to put away sin by the sacrifice of Himself. (Hebrews 9:26)
55. That if you confess with your mouth the Lord Jesus and believe in your heart that God has raised Him from the dead, you will be saved. (Romans 10:9)
56. But God demonstrates His own love toward us, in that while we were still sinners, Christ died for us. (Romans 5:8)

Testing for the Ultimate Authority

Test all things; hold fast what is good. (1 Thessalonians 5:21)

"Jesus was a good teacher, but he wasn't God."

"Death isn't the end. You come back again as someone else, based on how you lived your life."

"God used millions of years to create life and the universe."

If you're witnessing to someone, or even having a discussion with a fellow Christian, you may need to quickly perform a "foundational test" to effectively engage with their false ideas (or to determine if they are false!). This test asks, "Where is his argument really rooted?" In other words, what are the basic presuppositions behind what that person believes? Who or what is his ultimate authority?

And this isn't just for unbelievers. Many Christians say God and His Word are the ultimate and supreme authority, but in practice, they abandon that authority. We encounter this all the time at Answers in Genesis.

Seminary professors or pastors claim to believe in biblical authority and inerrancy but then turn around and deny God's clear Word in Genesis, adding evolution and millions of years into Scripture. When we put their words through "the authority test," it becomes obvious God's Word isn't really their authority, man is.

But why do so many Christians abandon the authority of God's Word in practice? Well, they've been influenced (probably without realizing it!) by the religion of our day: humanism. Yes, we must all be constantly on guard against false ideas regardless of their origin (1 Peter 5:8[1]). But why is the pull of humanism so strong that even Christians fall for it?

Influence of Humanism

Humanism is really a trap as old as the garden! In Genesis 3 Satan tempted Eve to eat the fruit of the tree by appealing to her own wisdom, questioning God's Word, and planting seeds of doubt. The result was she and Adam elevated their thinking—and the thinking of the serpent—above the clear Word of God. It was an attack on the authority of God's Word! And that's what humanism, in all its different forms, is.

In the religion of humanism, humans are essentially placed on top with everything else below. So, in this religion, God would be lower than man—or there is really no God at all. In other words, man is seen as supreme.

Aside from biblical Christianity, all religions are humanistic because they have elevated man, whether an ancient sage, a false prophet, or a man-made god, to supersede what God says in His Word. But in our Western culture *secular* forms of humanism are dominant.

Secular humanism really began taking hold in the Western world with the widespread rejection of God as the authority beginning about 200 or so years ago. Since then, humanism has become the dominant religion in universities, governments, and state schools in many parts of the world and is directly opposed to biblical authority. Since it's widely taught in schools, beginning at very young ages, it's no surprise that younger generations start with mankind as the authority.

1. Be sober, be vigilant; because your adversary the devil walks about like a roaring lion, seeking whom he may devour. (1 Peter 5:8)

God Is the Authority

As we've seen throughout this book, contrary to what the world believes, God, being the Creator and Sustainer of all things, is the ultimate authority in all matters. Consider God's Word:

> *All Scripture is given by inspiration of God, and is profitable for doctrine, for reproof, for correction, for instruction in righteousness, that the man of God may be complete, thoroughly equipped for every good work. I charge you therefore before God and the Lord Jesus Christ, who will judge the living and the dead at His appearing and His kingdom: Preach the word! Be ready in season and out of season. Convince, rebuke, exhort, with all longsuffering and teaching. For the time will come when they will not endure sound doctrine, but according to their own desires, because they have itching ears, they will heap up for themselves teachers; and they will turn their ears away from the truth, and be turned aside to fables. But you be watchful in all things, endure afflictions, do the work of an evangelist, fulfill your ministry.* (2 Timothy 3:16–4:5)

God determines what is right or wrong. Therefore, Scripture is useful for rebuking and correcting. Individuals, families, and governing authorities in various cultures (even humanistic ones) can and often do get laws and rules for civil life correct (e.g., Romans 2:15[2]), but this is because they are borrowing from what God has determined is right and wrong.

As we read above, the Bible reveals that there will be a time when people no longer adhere to "sound doctrine" but will turn aside from truth. In other words, one consequence of them heaping up teachers to tell them what they want to hear, is they will decide right and wrong based on their own desires. When one raises up his own desires to be the authority, this is humanism! It's when humans think they can sit in authority over God.

This turning aside to fables by the teaching of "ear-ticklers" is exactly what is happening with universities, schools, social media, and even many pastors and why Christians need to be exceptionally discerning lest they be led astray to fables by humanism instead of resting on Scripture.

---

2. Who show the work of the law written in their hearts, their conscience also bearing witness, and between themselves their thoughts accusing or else excusing them. (Romans 2:15)

The Authority Test

So what is "the authority test?" It's a way to honor 1 Thessalonians 5:21: "Test all things; hold fast what is good." God helps us think through the issues, using the standards of Scripture, to determine what is good and right. When we know what that is, we should hold fast to it.

And, as you search for truth in the Scriptures, remember what my father always told me: if something between Scripture and science (or any other "authority") doesn't agree, it's Scripture, not the other, that is correct. So go back to the passage, ensure you are properly interpreting it in light of the context and the genre, using Scripture to interpret Scripture, and if you are sure of your interpretation, go with God's Word—it's never wrong! Sometimes science just needs to catch up with biblical truth. In other words, let God interpret God, so that our fallible thinking doesn't interfere. (This is called the historical-grammatical approach when dealing with hermeneutics, the science of interpretation).

Using the following authority test can play a big part in the process of thinking through the issues. The authority test is this:

> Does the idea/statement/presupposition that I am confronted with have *man* as the ultimate authority or the *God* of the Bible as the ultimate authority? Are man's thoughts exalted above God's Word, or is the Word of God honored?

This authority test can be used two ways:

1. To better yourself by realizing where humanism has infiltrated your life and accordingly changing to align with God's Word (e.g., 2 Corinthians 3:5[3], 13:5[4])
2. To recognize when others are thinking "humanistically" and being able to reveal that fallacy to prepare to refute it (e.g., 2 Corinthians 10:3–6[5])

Brief Examples in Scripture

We see examples in Scripture where God's authority was reduced and man's ideas were raised up to be greater than what God said. Here's just a few:

3. **Adam and Eve** (Genesis 3): God's Word to Adam was clear (Genesis 2:17[6]). But when the woman was presented with two different options (what God said and what the serpent said), she raised her thoughts, based on what she saw and desired, up to be the authority on the subject of the fruit of the tree of the knowledge of good and evil. Eve, followed by her husband, was first to exhibit this humanistic trait.

---

3. Not that we are sufficient of ourselves to think of anything as being from ourselves, but our sufficiency is from God. (2 Corinthians 3:5)
4. Examine yourselves as to whether you are in the faith. Test yourselves. Do you not know yourselves, that Jesus Christ is in you? — unless indeed you are disqualified. (2 Corinthians 13:5)
5. For though we walk in the flesh, we do not war according to the flesh. For the weapons of our warfare are not carnal but mighty in God for pulling down strongholds, casting down arguments and every high thing that exalts itself against the knowledge of God, bringing every thought into captivity to the obedience of Christ, and being ready to punish all disobedience when your obedience is fulfilled. (2 Corinthians 10:3–6)
6. "But of the tree of the knowledge of good and evil you shall not eat, for in the day that you eat of it you shall surely die." (Genesis 2:17)

4. **Cain** (Genesis 4:1–12): Cain's sacrifice didn't mimic the sacrifice of an animal as God had shown his parents when He made for them garments of skin as a covering for their sin (Genesis 3:21[7]). Cain's sacrifice, for this or other reasons, was not acceptable compared to Abel's, who did offer an animal sacrifice. God advised Cain not to be angry and to do what was right, yet Cain did not listen to God, and, in his anger over God's authority to determine what is and what is not acceptable, went out and killed his brother Abel, violating God's transcendent law against murder. So, Cain raised up his own thoughts to be greater than God's by rejecting them. Once again, humanist thinking.

5. **Saul** (1 Samuel 15): Instead of listening to God's command to destroy everything after a battle, King Saul decided to keep back what he considered the best animal plunder to supposedly sacrifice to God. Saul sinfully decided not to take God seriously and lift up his own thoughts, and "good intentions," as greater than God's command.

6. **The Pharisees** (Matthew 12:38[8]): The Pharisees demanded a sign from Jesus. They placed themselves in authority by trying to force Jesus, the Almighty God, to submit to their wishes to prove Himself to them, thus putting themselves in authority over God.

Using the Test in Today's Culture

Christians should learn from these examples, understanding as I've emphasized throughout this book, that once you reduce God as the authority, then man's ideas, by default, become the authority—and that's empty and deceitful!

> *Beware lest anyone cheat you through philosophy and empty deceit, according to the tradition of men, according to the basic principles of the world, and not according to Christ.*
> (Colossians 2:8)

As Christians, we need to be able to discern if the ideas of men (even our own) are sitting in a position of authority over God's Word. Here are three examples:

7. And the LORD God made for Adam and for his wife garments of skins and clothed them. (Genesis 3:21, ESV)
8. Then some of the scribes and Pharisees answered, saying, "Teacher, we want to see a sign from You." (Matthew 12:38)

7. **Cults.** Many cults claim to believe the Word of God but then they add to it. In doing so, they are raising up man's words to be equal to or greater than God's Word. As soon as one refers to a book, magazine, person, organization/church denomination, etc. as having equal or greater authority than the Bible, that's a red flag that humanism has infiltrated.

8. **The deity of Christ.** John 1, Colossians 1, and Hebrews 1 are clear that Jesus Christ is the Creator God. Some people demean this and reduce the deity of Christ by radically reinterpreting these passages (among others). This is man sitting in authority over God's Word—again, not allowing Scripture to interpret Scripture.

9. **Millions of years.** You won't find the idea that the earth or universe is millions of years old in the Bible! A straightforward reading (supported by the context and other Scripture) gives six days for creation and 2,000 years from Adam to Abraham (based on the Genesis genealogies). With 2,000 more years from Abraham to Christ, and 2,000 more from Christ to us, there's only been about 6,000 years of history.

   The idea of millions and billions of years comes from man's ideas about the past. Secular scientists interpret the geologic layers as accumulating over millions of years, rejecting the global flood of Genesis which would've rapidly deposited these layers. When someone accepts millions of years, they are putting man's ideas over God's Word because they've been influenced by naturalism (which goes hand-in-hand with humanism). Rather than examining the evidence in the present in light of God's Word, they start with man's ideas, interpret the evidence through that lens, and then change the Bible! This is putting man as the authority, not God.

With these examples in mind, apply "the authority test" to these statements and see if you can spot the humanism:

1. "My pastor said that our denomination agrees that evolution and the Bible are compatible."

2. "The Bible doesn't mean a normal, 24-hour day in Genesis 1 because science says it is much longer."

With our first example, the person appealed to a pastor, who appealed to the specific denomination, which appealed to man's ideas about millions of years and evolution. Yes, there can be multiple levels of humanistic thinking before you get to the root!

In our second example, the person appealed to "science," but really he means a secular interpretation of scientific facts (using a reification fallacy no less!). We must use our God-given mind to reach logical conclusions, but if our minds interpret facts in such a way that our conclusion contradicts God's Word, then we must reject that conclusion and give God the benefit of the doubt. When we don't, we are guilty of humanistic thinking. We must allow God's Word to be the ultimate authority.

We must realize that when man tries to sit in authority over the Word of God, then he is trying to judge God. But God makes it clear that it is He and His Word that will judge us. My prayer is that each one of us will use "the authority test" on a daily basis to correct our thinking. This is one of the first steps to get back to biblical authority.

Testing Humanism and Witnessing

Now let's apply "the authority test" to some secular statements. Again, try to spot the humanism in these:

1. The paper from the latest scientific journal says dinosaurs and man didn't live at the same time.
2. Most secular scientists believe in evolution, so it must be true.
3. The Bible can't be true because it is full of contradictions.

In example #1, the scientific paper is given authority over the Bible's statement that on day 6, God created both man and land animals (which includes dinosaurs). Where did that paper come from? Fallible man.

In example #2, the speaker appealed to multiple humans (the majority of scientists) as an authority over God and implies consensus is the method by which we determine truth—but how often has that consensus changed? (Remember, the consensus in Noah's day was that there would be no Flood!)

In our final example, the person is sitting in authority over God's Word claiming there are contradictions (which there aren't[9]) and saying, in effect, that God is lying or can't get His facts straight in what He claims is

9. For more on this, see *Demolishing Supposed Bible Contradictions Vol. 1 and 2*, available at AnswersinGenesis.org.

His true, perfect, and complete Word (Revelation 22:18–19[10]; 2 Timothy 3:16–17[11]; 2 Timothy 2:15[12]; Romans 3:2[13]; Hebrews 4:12[14], etc.).

Following Up the Test in Practice

The authority test simply allows you to recognize the root of a belief system—either it goes back to God or it goes back to mankind. So what's the next step?

4. To reveal to that person the real religion/worldview that they believe or have been influenced by is humanism

5. To show the foundational problems with that view (i.e., faulty appeal to authority fallacy/misplaced authority fallacy/false authority fallacy)

6. To present what the Bible says and culminate with the gospel

Many people who think humanistically simply don't realize it. So, your first goal is to kindly reveal this to them. Perhaps challenge a humanistic worldview (in kindness) by asking questions about how they view the world and how their beliefs relate to things in reality. This is usually a non-threatening way to get people (Christian or not) to think about their beliefs more deeply because they probably haven't—especially the foundation for their belief system.

This also reveals problems with the foundation of humanism. For example, ask "why do people generally wear clothes?" The person may be a bit taken aback, but what this shows is that a humanistic view of the past

10. For I testify to everyone who hears the words of the prophecy of this book: If anyone adds to these things, God will add to him the plagues that are written in this book; and if anyone takes away from the words of the book of this prophecy, God shall take away his part from the Book of Life, from the holy city, and from the things which are written in this book. (Revelation 22:18–19)
11. See page 175.
12. Be diligent to present yourself approved to God, a worker who does not need to be ashamed, rightly dividing the word of truth. (2 Timothy 2:15)
13. Much in every way! Chiefly because to them were committed the oracles of God. (Romans 3:2)
14. For the word of God is living and powerful, and sharper than any two-edged sword, piercing even to the division of soul and spirit, and of joints and marrow, and is a discerner of the thoughts and intents of the heart. (Hebrews 4:12)

really doesn't explain the world. Ultimately, of course, clothing is a Christian concept that goes back to sin, shame, and sacrifice in Genesis 3.

Or ask about marriage. Where does the idea of marriage come from? (Ultimately, it comes from the Bible, too—beginning in Genesis.) Ask why death exists, if "right and wrong" exist, and what is the ultimate standard by which we judge what is right or wrong? Ask if truth exists. If so, what exactly is it? And then ask if truth is the same for everyone. Ask where the world and universe came from, where life came from, and so on.

A few questions like these should get the person thinking (without being "preachy"). What will likely happen, though, is that the person will reveal what he really believes about origins . . . which is probably a mixture of the big bang, long ages, and evolution, maybe with some spirituality—or even some Christianity—mixed in.

When some of that comes out, point out the areas in which they are thinking as a humanist (evolution, naturalism, long ages, big bang, etc. are subsets of humanism.) You may even have to explain it. Once they realize how humanism has influenced them, then proceed to point out that humans (or even that person individually) are really raising themselves up to be "gods" by placing themselves as the ultimate authority. Point out that humanism is really a polytheistic religion where each human is his own "god."

This should get through any humanist thinking, then you can show that the Bible does explain things like the origin of matter, space, time, marriage, clothing, morality, truth, and so on. This then leads to the gospel and an explanation of God's original perfect creation and the doctrine of sin (yes, it's our sin that has made the world like it is—full of death and suffering). Then share how Christ came to save us from sin and death.

While witnessing, remember to be kind and patient (e.g., 2 Timothy 2:24[15]). After all, we were enemies of the gospel ourselves at one point (Colossians 1:21[16]), but Jesus Christ was patient with us and performed the ultimate act of kindness on the Cross.

15. And a servant of the Lord must not quarrel but be gentle to all, able to teach, patient. (2 Timothy 2:24)
16. And you, who once were alienated and enemies in your mind by wicked works, yet now He has reconciled. (Colossians 1:21, NKJV)

21 Practical Micro-Refutations of False Worldview

Can you refute error?

Scripture calls Christians to refute (i.e., prove false) false views (e.g., 2 Corinthians 10:4–5[1]). And with just a little knowledge, you can usually refute false religions and beliefs easier than you'd think. As we've seen throughout this book, we can do this in two ways:

1. By using God's Word (the absolute standard). To use God's Word to refute false views, you have to know what it says! Start by knowing God's Word (this means reading, studying, and meditating on it).

   All other authorities are lesser authorities, so appealing to lesser authorities commits a false authority fallacy every time. Even so, sadly, because of our sinful hearts, many will still ignore the Bible's refutation of their religion and continue believing false beliefs.

---

1. For the weapons of our warfare are not of the flesh but have divine power to destroy strongholds. We destroy arguments and every lofty opinion raised against the knowledge of God, and take every thought captive to obey Christ. (2 Corinthians 10:4–5 ESV)

Nevertheless, if a religion, worldview, or belief system is inconsistent with God's Word or violates the *preconditions of intelligibility* that come from God's Word, then that view is false.

2. By showing that the religion or belief is fallacious within its own story or set of beliefs. There are three ways this can be done (remember the AIP analysis!). These religions can catch themselves in *arbitrariness, inconsistencies,* or by giving up their belief system to borrow from the Bible to make sense of things (the *preconditions of intelligibility*).

Refutation usually grabs people's attention by showing that their beliefs really are just sinking sand. And any *one* refutation of a false set of beliefs (e.g., worldview, philosophical system, or religion) is enough to refute the whole thing. It's that simple. So let's look at some "to-the-point" refutations in a practical way.

A Few Micro-Refutations

Materialism, a belief that asserts that all things that exist are made up of matter and energy, is itself not material or energy, but a nonmaterial *concept*. This means materialism cannot exist within materialism. Thus, materialism is self-defeating and refuted.

Eastern religions, like *Taoism* and *Hinduism*, have an impersonal "god" (e.g., *Brahman* or ultimate reality). How then can anyone know that this "god" is impersonal? After all, this "god" cannot communicate anything about itself to man since communication is personal. This is arbitrary, to say the least, and self-refuting.

Agnosticism, which claims that one cannot know if God exists, has no basis for the existence of knowledge and, thus, is stuck in a catch-22. The agnostic cannot even know if he can or cannot know if knowledge exists. Thus, he cannot even know if he is in a position to determine if God exists or not. Thus, it is inconsistent and self-contradictory.

The Koran (Qur'an) affirms that the Bible is true and the Word of God[2] but then contradicts it,[3] thus showing that the Koran has erred. The Koran

2. See Surah 2:40–42, 126, 136, 285; 3:3, 71, 93; 4:47, 136; 5:47–51, 69, 71–72; 6:91; 10:37, 94; 21:7; 29:45–46; 35:31; 46:11.
3. See Surah 3:35–36; 4:157, 5:17, 5:73–75, 116, 19:27–28; 66:12.

says that no one can change the Word of God (Surah 6:34, 10:64) but then claims the Bible has been changed (Surah 2:75, 101; 3:70, 78, 187; 4:46), though there is no textual witness of such an occurrence. Then the Koran states that *its* words *have* changed (Surah 2:106; 15:90–93;[4] 16:101). Thus, the Koran contradicts both the Bible and itself.

Atheists say there is no God. To make this claim, the atheist must be omnipresent to observe that God does not exist in the past, present, or future heavenly or physical realms (recall the disproof of atheism chapter); the atheist must be omnipotent to have the power to stop an all-powerful God from taking His place as God; and, lastly, the atheist must have all knowledge (omniscience) to finally know for sure that God doesn't exist. Therefore, the atheist must be an omnipresent, omnipotent, and omniscient "god" to say there is no omnipresent, omnipotent, omniscient God. They must have the attributes of God to claim God doesn't exist. Thus, the atheistic position is self-refuting.

Atheists continually attack God, whom they lump together with mythical persons like the Easter bunny, the tooth fairy, and Santa Claus in their books, articles, lectures, memes, billboards, and so on—yet they don't spend the effort to do this with the Easter bunny, tooth fairy, and Santa Claus. This is arbitrary and inconsistent. When it comes to suppression of the truth (Romans 1), actions speak louder than words.

Naturalism, which is a belief that nature (all that is physical) is all that exists, is itself not part of nature—*being conceptual and nonphysical*. Thus, naturalism stands opposed to naturalism. This is inconsistent and self-refuting.

Those in *relativism* criticize the absolute truth of Christianity by arguing that "absolute truth doesn't exist." But are they absolutely sure about that? Just ask them why they are professing an *absolute truth* about absolute truth not existing. It's that simple to refute.

At this point, I want you to notice something: we were using their own arguments against them (like an internal critique). But each of these worldviews was already proven false because God in His Word has disagreed with them. So they are false on both fronts.

4. Sam Shamoun, "The Quran Testifies to Its Own Textual Corruption," Answering Islam, http://www.answering-islam.org/authors/shamoun/corruption_testimony.html.

The Illogical Sequence

In our culture many false beliefs are taught as fact in public schools to generations of students. In most of these schools, Christianity has come under direct attack, and there has been a concerted effort to remove God and His Word and evaporate any teachings of Scripture from classrooms.

But if state schools really want to get all semblance of Christianity out of the classroom (they say they want religion out of the classroom but they don't—they want their religion of secular humanism in the classroom!), they should stop having weekends (which are really Christian holidays based on the Sabbath and Lord's Day) and stop taking holidays ("*holy* days," which are predicated on a *holy* God). Animals don't take weekends or holidays off.

In fact, education itself is a Christian concept from the pages of Scripture (e.g., Deuteronomy 6:7[5]; Proverbs 22:6[6]). The fact that educational institutions exist in the first place is predicated on the Bible being true! Rabbits don't set up educational systems and you won't see a group of beavers forming elementary schools, high schools, and colleges.

Why don't we see a constant barrage of atheist lawsuits to rid our school system of weekends and other Christian holidays? It is very "Christian" for these schools to retain these Christian holidays (and to agree educational institutions should exist!)—but they give up their own professed worldview to do so.

State schools and universities generally teach children the evolutionary view that they are animals, that there is no ultimate right and wrong, and there is no God. However, when these same kids do drugs, cheat, vandalize, rape, dishonor faculty and staff, get drunk, shoot their classmates, and live like animals, they are chastised for not "behaving" (i.e., acting with Christian morality). Note the inconsistency!

Likewise, those who identify as transgender (often because they've been heavily influenced by social media and their secular education!) are offended that Christians like myself don't accept them for "who they are," when…they don't accept themselves for who they are (hence, the

5. You shall teach them diligently to your children, and shall talk of them when you sit in your house, and when you walk by the way, and when you lie down, and when you rise. (Deuteronomy 6:7, ESV)
6. Train up a child in the way he should go; even when he is old he will not depart from it. (Proverbs 22:6, ESV)

attempted transition from who God created them to be!)! And, furthermore, they don't accept me for who I am (a double standard). Are they repentant over offending me by their actions? No. This is inconsistent and thus false.

Yes, all false worldviews are internally inconsistent. To refute these wrong views, immerse yourself in the Bible and its teachings—that's of utmost importance (Hebrews 4:12[7]). God's Word is the most powerful refutation for the Word of God will be the judge (John 12:48[8]). But it's also great to know some easy refutations of other worldviews and religions so you can help humble the unbeliever and trust God will use His Word to accomplish salvation.

7. For the word of God is living and powerful, and sharper than any two-edged sword, piercing even to the division of soul and spirit, and of joints and marrow, and is a discerner of the thoughts and intents of the heart. (Hebrews 4:12)
8. He who rejects Me, and does not receive My words, has that which judges him — the word that I have spoken will judge him in the last day. (John 12:48)

The Bible vs. Other Alleged Holy Books

How do we know the Bible's true when there's so many "holy books" to chose from—like the Upanishads, Confucius's writings, Book of Mormon, Vedas, Studies in the Scriptures (Charles Russell) and the Qur'an?

This line-up looks like a buffet where you pick and choose what you want, doesn't it? And that's what many people do! They pick based on what they think is the truth. But if you are the authority on the truthfulness of a religious book, then God (or god/gods) *cannot* be.

In other words, if someone argues that God is the absolute authority by appealing to his own opinions as the ultimate authority, then that person refutes himself. It sounds complicated but, once again, it's either man is the authority or God is.

So let's look at this issue in more detail.

Some "Holy Books" Do Not Claim to Be the Word of God

This might surprise you, but many "holy books" aren't holy, and they admit it! In other words, they do not claim to be the Word of God. They are like any other writing.

For instance, take ancient Hindu writings. The Vedas, Upanishads, or even the Bhagavad Gita are not the revealed word of their god, Brahman (other gods in Hinduism are considered manifestations of Brahman). Brahman is not a personal god, so revelation (i.e., communication) from Brahman is not a possibility since communication is a personal attribute.

These alleged holy writings are merely the opinions of their ancient sages on the subject. The alleged holy books of Hinduism are nothing more than errant books of man, nothing that should be confused with the inerrant Word of God. Any writing of an alleged *impersonal* god (e.g., New Age, Scientology, Taoism, etc.) is in the same camp.

Obviously, any book about religions that have no god (e.g., secular religions or many moralistic religions) cannot be confused as the Word of God either. So there goes any Buddhist, Confucianist, Epicurean, Stoic, and atheistic writing. Believe it or not, this eliminates Satanism's writings, too (LaVey's *The Satanic Bible* and *The Devil's Notebook* for example). LaVey was actually an atheist arguing for atheism in the books!

Multi-god systems like Germanic or Greek mythologies, Shinto, and so forth are little more than ancestor worship where people were elevated to a god-like status. Oden and Thor, for example, are listed in ancient genealogies and were likely real people who later had god-like attributes attached to them. Again, these are all merely the arbitrary and fallible opinions of man any way you look at them.

Pagan religions like witchcraft, voodoo, and animism do not have a supreme god who reveals his or her will. There are no unified, absolute scriptures for paganism. This explains why there are such varied beliefs among pagans. It comes down to the mind of mankind.

A deistic god generally remains distant from his creation, so there is no need for this alleged god to communicate with beings within his creation. So, according to the story of most deists, there should be no Word of God!

Other "Holy Books" Agree the Bible Is True!

Other alleged holy books or prophets often agree the Bible is true but usually want to add their own ideas or interpretations to it.

Charles Taze Russell, the founder and supposed prophet behind the Jehovah's Witnesses, affirmed that the Bible is true. Russell just opted to *add* his works to it. The Watch Tower Bible and Tract Society (Jehovah's Witnesses) has continued in the same trend as Russell.

Founder of the Mormons (Church of Jesus Christ of Latter Day Saints), alleged prophet Joseph Smith, and subsequent Mormon leadership, also agree that the Bible is true (insofar as it is accurately translated), although Smith attempted to *add* the Book of Mormon, the Pearl of Great Price, and the Doctrines and Covenants as Scripture.

The alleged prophetess behind the Seventh Day Adventists (SDA), Ellen G. White, agreed the Bible is true, though her writings were seen by many early SDAs as inerrant—an *addition* to Scripture. Encouragingly, we see many SDAs today who no longer hold Ellen White in such high esteem and now see the Bible as the *sole* source of doctrine.

Even Muhammad, the prophet of Islam, agreed the Bible is true and this appears several times in the Qur'an (e.g., Surah 2:40–42, 126, 136, 285; 3:3, 71, 93; 4:47, 136; 5:47–51, 69, 71–72; 6:91; 10:37, 94; 21:7; 29:45–46; 35:31; 46:11–12). But the Qur'an was seen as the true revelation.

Within Roman Catholicism, they agree the Bible is true, but then try to *add* the Apocryphal books, along with papal/ecumenical authority (this is a response called an "infallible pronouncement" on faith and moral issues if they are called into question).

The Jews agreed on much of the Scripture (Old Testament) but then *add* the Talmud, Mishna, etc. (oral traditions put to writing beginning about A.D. 200) while rejecting the New Testament.

This list could continue, but the point is that many who have professed additional writings from God still agree that the Bible is true. So the issue with them is not the Bible, there's little dispute there; the issue is their additions that need to be judged and tested by the Bible (previous Scripture).

	Bible is true?	But wants to add...
Mormons	Yes	Book of Mormon, the Pearl of Great Price, and the Doctrines and Covenants
Jehovah's Witnesses	Yes	Studies in the Scripture, Watchtower, and Awake
Muslims	Yes	Qur'an and Hadith
Seventh-Day Adventists	Yes	Ellen G. White's writings
Roman Catholics	Yes	Apocrypha and Papal authority
Jews	Most (OT)	Talmud (Traditions)
Orthodox Christians	Yes	Some Apocrypha and Patriarchal authority
Syncretists	Yes	Humanistic Origins (various degrees of evolution)
Bahá'ís	Yes	Qur'an and Bahaullah's writings and his sons, modern prophets and the House of Justice
Biblical Christians	Yes	**Nothing**

This overview shows that the Bible has very little competition when you actually look at the issue. It is by no means a buffet of scriptures! The questions are, "Is the Bible true?" and "Does the competition even come close?"

The Authority of Scripture

As we've seen, the God of the Bible is absolute by His very nature. He is the ultimate authority on all things. By extension, His Word is the ultimate authority on all things.

God, being the ultimate and final authority, can only reveal Himself by final and absolute authority. In other words, there is no other authority to "prove" God and His Word as all other authorities are *lesser* than God.

This is why *no person, myself included*, is in a position to prove God and His Word. If I appealed to my arbitrary opinions on God or His Word, I would be a lesser authority than God—being a fallible and imperfect man.

As we saw in earlier chapters, we can't even use logic to "prove God" because even logic is dependent upon God existing and Him being the ultimate authority. In other words, it's a lesser authority; all things (man, logic, angels, governments, etc.) are lesser than God, and thus lesser in authority than God and His Word.

So only God is left in the position to prove Himself and His Word[1] and He did it with the first few words of Genesis.

> *In the beginning God...* (Genesis 1:1)

This initial phrase is the foundation of the rest of Genesis 1:1. Genesis 1:1 is the foundation for the rest of Genesis 1–11. Genesis 1–11 is the foundation for the rest of the Bible and for our doctrine, theology, worldview, the gospel, and, well, everything!

The Bible, from Genesis to Revelation, is equal to God in authority and is our absolute starting point for all matters, even the existence of God.[2] Any objector would be a lesser authority and, therefore, not in a position to usurp the authority of God.

"But the Bible Was Written by Mere Men!"

So what about the objection that the Bible was written by men? This is a common argument from those who reject God's existence (and even many progressive "Christians" today). They claim the Bible is really no different from any other book because men wrote it.

---

1. Some might object and appeal to logic that this is a circular argument, thus fallacious. However, circular arguments are *valid* logically. What makes a circular argument fallacious is when it is an *arbitrary* circle. God, being absolute and final, is non-arbitrary. Thus it is valid and sound, so one cannot appeal to this being a fallacious argument.
2. If you recall Chapter 9, this is called the Transcendental Argument for the Existence of God (TAG). It is not an argument per se but is the foundation that makes all argumentation possible.

Now, when it comes to the authorship of the Bible, of course men were involved—the Bible doesn't try to hide this! Paul wrote letters to early churches, and these became Scripture. David wrote many of the Psalms, Moses wrote the Pentateuch (the first five books of the Bible), and so on. In fact, it is estimated that over 40 different human authors were involved.[3]

But this isn't the real issue. The real issue is whether God had any involvement in the authorship of the Bible because, when someone claims that the Bible was written by men, they really mean to say it was written by men *without God's involvement.*

Now think about that for a moment—that is an absolute statement that reveals the objector is claiming to be…transcendent. For a person to validate the claim that God did not inspire the human authors of the Bible means he must be omniscient, omnipresent, and omnipotent to know this is the case!

1. *Omniscient*: This person is claiming to be an all-knowing authority on the subject of God's inspiration in order to refute God's claim that Scripture was inspired by Him (2 Timothy 3:16[4]).
2. *Omnipresent*: This person is claiming that he was present, both spiritually and physically, to observe that God had no part in aiding any of the biblical authors as they penned Scripture.
3. *Omnipotent*: This person is claiming that, had God tried to inspire the biblical authors, they had the power to stop such an action.

So, the person claiming that the Bible was merely written by men is claiming to be God since these three attributes belong to God alone. It's humanism vs. Christianity again! People who make such claims (perhaps unwittingly) are claiming that *they* are the ultimate authority over God and are trying to convince others that God is *subservient* to them.

When someone makes this claim, you can point out their outlandish claim to be God by asking some questions,

> "Do you really believe that you are omnipresent? The only way for you to make your point that God had no involvement would be if you were omnipresent."

---

3. Josh McDowell, *A Ready Defense,* Thomas Nelson Publishers, Nashville, Tennessee, 1993, p. 27.
4. All Scripture is given by inspiration of God, and is profitable for doctrine, for reproof, for correction, for instruction in righteousness. (2 Timothy 3:16)

Or "How is it that you are powerful enough to stop God from inspiring the authors? And since the only way to refute the fact that God inspired the Bible is to use attributes of God such as omnipresence, omnipotence, and omniscience, you'd have to be God!"

Or "How do you know that God was not involved?" (The person will probably respond by saying "well, because the Bible is full of contradictions," or something like that. You can then address that issue – and I find if you ask for an alleged contradiction, you'll rarely get a specific example. The person is just regurgitating something they heard online.)

Other responses include undercutting the entire position by pointing out that any type of reasoning apart from the Bible is merely arbitrary. So, the person trying to make a logical argument against the claims of the Bible (i.e., that God inspired the authors) is doing so only because he or she is assuming (though unintentionally) the Bible is true and that logic and truth exist! It is good to point out these types of presuppositions and inconsistencies.[5]

Someone may respond and say, "What if I claim that Shakespeare was inspired by God? Then you would have to be omniscient, omnipresent, and omnipotent to refute it."

But it's irrelevant *for me* to be omniscient, omnipresent, and omnipotent to refute such a claim. God, who is omniscient, omnipresent, and omnipotent, has already refuted this claim in the Bible. Nowhere has God authenticated Shakespeare's writings as Scripture, unlike Christ, the Creator God's (John 1; Colossians 1; Hebrews 1), approval of the Old Testament prophetic works and the New Testament apostolic works. The cap of the canon is already sealed.[6]

A Presuppositional Authority

God exists, and His Word, the Bible, is the truth. This is the starting point.

---

5. Jason Lisle, "Put the Bible Down," Answers in Genesis, December 5, 2008, www.answersingenesis.org/articles/2008/12/05/feedback-put-the-bible-down.
6. "A Look at the Canon" Answers in Genesis, January 23, 2008, www.answersingenesis.org/articles/aid/v3/n1/look-at-the-canon.

God simply opens the Bible with a statement of His existence and says His Word is flawless (Genesis 1:1[7]; Proverbs 30:5[8]). The Bible bluntly claims to be the truth (Psalm 119:160[9]), and Christ repeated this claim (John 17:17[10]).

In fact, if God had tried to prove that He existed or that His Word was flawless by any other means, then any evidence or proof would be greater than God and His Word—which would be contradictory to God's nature.

God knows that nothing is greater than He (e.g., Hebrews 6:13[11]) and by extension, His Word, and therefore He doesn't stoop to our carnal desires for such proofs. Instead God offers proof by the impossibility of the contrary (more on this in a moment).

The Bible also teaches us to have faith that God exists and that having faith pleases Him (Hebrews 11:6). So we're on the right track if we start with God's Word.

Additional or Competitive "Holy Books"?

Scripture comes from God, and God cannot contradict Himself. If God were to contradict Himself, then all knowledge would be arbitrary and nothing would be trustworthy or could even really be known. Thus, when God reveals Himself, it will not be in contradiction.

Previous Scripture Is the Judge of Latter Scripture

Furthermore, when God revealed more about Himself in subsequent Scripture, it was consistent with the previous revelation. New revelation built on previous Scripture as the *previous* judged the latter (newer Scripture). The Holy Spirit revealed this through Moses (e.g., Deuteronomy 13, Acts 1:16[12]).

---

7. In the beginning God created the heavens and the earth. (Genesis 1:1)
8. Every word of God proves true; he is a shield to those who take refuge in him. (Proverbs 30:5, ESV)
9. The entirety of Your word is truth, and every one of Your righteous judgments endures forever. (Psalm 119:160)
10. Sanctify them by Your truth. Your word is truth. (John 17:17)
11. For when God made a promise to Abraham, because He could swear by no one greater, He swore by Himself. (Hebrews 6:13)
12. Men and brethren, this Scripture had to be fulfilled, which the Holy Spirit spoke before by the mouth of David concerning Judas, who became a guide to those who arrested Jesus. (Acts 1:16)

This is why the New Testament uses the Old Testament to prove itself (e.g., Acts 17:10–11[13]). For example, Jesus, the Apostles, and others in the New Testament used the Old Testament witness as their proof of Jesus as the Messiah. The Old Testament judged the New Testament. The New Testament was not contradictory to the Old Testament, but instead fulfilled what the Old Testament was looking toward and built upon its foundation.

A red flag should go up when someone says that previous Scripture (e.g., the Old or New Testament) should be judged based on their alleged "new Scripture." They have it backward. Imagine if the new were to judge the old, instead of the old judging the new—anyone could claim new revelation from God and put themselves into a position of authority greater than God! And many have tried to do just that.

For example, Mormons say the Book of Mormon and other Mormon writings are the authority and the Bible is secondary based on the interpretation and translation of the Bible according to Mormon teaching. They place the latter Mormon writings in a superior position to the previous (Bible).

The Jehovah's Witnesses do the same thing. The Bible is secondary to *their* writings and subject to the Watch Tower Organization and Charles Russell's view of the Scripture. They have the latter in a superior position to the previous.

Islam fairs the same with the Qur'an in a higher position than the Bible. Again, this is back to front.

Ellen G. White's writings are more of the same; her writings are viewed as the authority, and the Bible takes a secondary role, being interpreted based upon her view of the Bible.

At the very least, if these alleged prophets viewed their works as equal to the Bible, then they should have taught that their works were equal to but not greater than the previous! Instead, they always elevate their own alleged revelations to supersede the Bible—because the Bible contradicts their writings! This elevation of man is a red flag to anyone using "the authority test."

13. Then the brethren immediately sent Paul and Silas away by night to Berea. When they arrived, they went into the synagogue of the Jews. These were more fair-minded than those in Thessalonica, in that they received the word with all readiness, and searched the Scriptures daily to find out whether these things were so. (Acts 17:10–11)

Sadly, this method of taking the new as authoritative and neglecting the old in light of it is nothing new. Even Jesus had to deal with this!

The Jews of Jesus' time held to the traditions of the elders (later written down and called the *Talmud*—either the *Babylonian Talmud* or the *Jerusalem Talmud*) as superior to Moses and the Old Testament prophets. In light of these traditions, they reinterpreted the Old Testament in ways that destroyed the meanings of passages and made useless the commands of God.

The New Testament did not do that. The New Testament apostles consistently argued their case *based* upon the Old Testament and gave equal authority to their New Testament Scripture as a fulfillment to the Old Testament. The New Testament books were not seen as superior documents to the Old Testament which now need reinterpreting.

The same occurred throughout the Old Testament. When Old Testament prophets spoke, "thus says the Lord," they did not say their writings were superior and that Moses now needed to be seen as secondary or reinterpreted based on their new revelation. No, their prophetic works were seen as building on the foundation of Moses.

Previous Scripture is to be used to judge latter Scripture. When an alleged new prophet claims the opposite, they stand in contradiction to Bible and, thus, are false prophets.

God Will Not Contradict Himself

In the Bible, we read that God cannot lie (Titus 1:2[14]; Hebrews 6:18[15]). This is significant because it means that God's Word will never contradict itself. Though skeptics have alleged that there are contradictions in the Bible, every such claim has been refuted.[16] This is what we would expect if God's Word were perfect.[17]

14. In hope of eternal life which God, who cannot lie, promised before time began. (Titus 1:2)
15. That by two immutable things, in which it is impossible for God to lie, we might have strong consolation, who have fled for refuge to lay hold of the hope set before us. (Hebrews 6:18)
16. There are websites and books dedicated to this subject. To get started, I suggest *Demolishing Supposed Bible Contradictions,* Volumes 1 and 2.
17. Keep in mind a crucial point here. *If* the Bible were not true and not from God, then contradictions are acceptable! It is from a biblical perspective that contradictions are a bad thing. If a secular worldview were correct (no God and no Word of God), why not contradict yourself?

Yet the world is filled with other "religious writings" that claim divine origin or that have been treated as equal to or higher than the Bible on matters of truth or guidelines for living. In other words, these writings are treated as a final authority over the Bible.

Any religious writing that claims divine inspiration or authority equal to the Bible can't be from God if it has any contradictions: contradictions with the Bible, contradictions within itself, or contradictions with reality.

So we can test any religious writing by comparing what it says to the Bible. When the Bible was being written and Paul was preaching to the Bereans (Acts 17:11[18]), he commended them for checking his words against the Scriptures that were already written. If someone claims that a book is of divine origin, we should be Bereans ourselves and test it to confirm whether it agrees with the 66 books of the Bible. Paul's writings, of course, were Scripture (2 Peter 3:16[19]).

Religious books, such as Islam's *Koran* (Qur'an), Mormonism's *Book of Mormon*, and Hinduism's *Vedas*, contradict the Bible, so they cannot be Scripture. For example,

- the *Koran* in two chapters (Surah 4:171 and 23:91) says God had no son, but the Bible is clear that Jesus is the only begotten Son of God (Matthew 26:63–64[20])
- the Book of Mormon says in Moroni 8:8 that children are not sinners, but the Bible teaches that children are sinful, even from birth (Psalm 51:5[21]). *The Book of Mormon*, prior to the 1981 change, says that Native Americans will turn white when they convert to Mormonism (2 Nephi 30:6).

18. These were more fair-minded than those in Thessalonica, in that they received the word with all readiness, and searched the Scriptures daily to find out whether these things were so. (Acts 17:11)
19. As also in all his epistles, speaking in them of these things, in which are some things hard to understand, which untaught and unstable people twist to their own destruction, as they do also the rest of the Scriptures. (2 Peter 3:16)
20. But Jesus kept silent. And the high priest answered and said to Him, "I put You under oath by the living God: Tell us if You are the Christ, the Son of God!" Jesus said to him, "It is as you said. Nevertheless, I say to you, hereafter you will see the Son of Man sitting at the right hand of the Power, and coming on the clouds of heaven." (Matthew 26:63–64)
21. Behold, I was brought forth in iniquity, And in sin my mother conceived me. (Psalm 51:5)

- Few would dispute that the *Vedas* and other writings in Hinduism are starkly different (thus contradictory) from the Bible as previously discussed. None of the apocryphal books of Catholicism or Orthodoxy claim inspiration from God. One apocryphal book *Maccabees* (1 Maccabees 9:27, 4:46, and 14:41) points out that no prophets were in the land and hadn't been for some time. Since prophets were the mouthpieces of God, how can these books, written during this time that prophets weren't present in Israel, be the Word of God?
- The Talmud, which is "the traditions of the elders, tradition of the fathers," "law of the fathers," or "tradition of men," was strictly opposed by Jesus and the New Testament (e.g. Matthew 15:2–6; Mark 7:3–13; Acts 22:3[22])

Also, such religious writings contain contradictions within themselves that are unanswerable without logical gymnastics. For example, in the *Koran*, one passage says Jesus will be with God in paradise (Surah 3:45) and another states that He will be in hell for being worshiped by Christians (Surah 21:98).

If these writings were truly from God, such discrepancies couldn't exist.

Chart of contradictions with some popular alleged new Scripture and the Bible

	Bible	New "Scripture" Claims
Koran (Qur'an)	Jesus is God who became a man as well (Colossians 2:9)	Jesus is not God (Surah 5:17, 5:75)
Koran (Qur'an)	Jesus was crucified (1 Peter 2:24)	Jesus was not crucified (Surah 4:157)
Koran (Qur'an)	The Holy Spirit is God (Acts 5:3–4; 2 Corinthians 3:15–17)	The Holy Spirit is the created angel Gabriel (Surah 2:97, 16:102)
Book of Mormon	Salvation is by faith through grace apart from works (Ephesians 2:8–9)	Salvation is by grace and works (2 Nephi 25:23)
Book of Mormon	One God exists (Deuteronomy 6:4; 1 Chronicles 17:20; 1 Timothy 2:5)	Multiple gods exist (Doctrine and Covenants, Section 121:32, 132:18–20)

22. I am indeed a Jew, born in Tarsus of Cilicia, but brought up in this city at the feet of Gamaliel, taught according to the strictness of our fathers' law, and was zealous toward God as you all are today. (Acts 22:3)

	Bible	New "Scripture" Claims
Jehovah's Witnesses	Jesus is the Creator God (John 1:1–3; Hebrews 1:1–9; Colossians 1:15–19) and distinguished from angels (Hebrews 1:4–8)	Jesus is the created angel, Michael[23]
Jehovah's Witnesses	Hell is a place of eternal torment for those who do not receive Christ (e.g., Daniel 12:2; Matthew 25:41–46; Mark 9:43–48; John 3:36; 2 Thessalonians 1:9; Revelation 14:9–11,)	Hell is not a place of eternal torment[24]
Jehovah's Witnesses	God created in six, 24-hour days as defined by an evening and a morning in Genesis 1 and rested on the seventh day (Genesis 1:1–2:3; Exodus 20:11; Exodus 31:15–17)	God created in 49,000 years with each day being 7,000 years in duration (Charles Russell, *Studies in the Scripture*, Volume 6, p. 19)

False Prophecy

A prophet is one who claims to speak for God, often foretelling events. The Holy Spirit, speaking through Moses, writes,

> *But the prophet who presumes to speak a word in My name, which I have not commanded him to speak, or who speaks in the name of other gods, that prophet shall die. And if you say in your heart, "How shall we know the word which the LORD has not spoken?" – when a prophet speaks in the name of the LORD, if the thing does not happen or come to pass, that is the thing which the LORD has not spoken; the prophet has spoken it presumptuously; you shall not be afraid of him.* (Deuteronomy 18:20–22)

Matthew 7:15–20 reiterates a warning against false prophets. How have the alleged prophets since the Bible fared?

23. "Who Is Michael the Archangel," JW.org, accessed August 30, 2016, https://www.jw.org/en/publications/books/bible-teach/who-is-michael-the-archangel-jesus/.
24. "What Is Hell? Is It a Place of Eternal Torment?" JW.org, accessed August 30, 2016, https://www.jw.org/en/bible-teachings/questions/what-is-hell/.

Islam

In the Hadith tradition of Sunan Abu Dawud, Book 37, Number 4281–4283, Muhammad claimed that the Antichrist (*Dajjal*) was supposed to come forth six months after the conquest of Constantinople by the Muslims. At the same time, Medina (Yathrib) would be left in ruins.

The Muslim conquest was much later than Muhammad's day, finally occurring in May of A.D. 1453. But no Antichrist ascended in November of 1453 and Medina was not left in ruins.

Mormons (Church of Jesus Christ of Latter-Day Saints)

The Mormons have not fared any better.

> Yea, the word of the Lord concerning his church, established in the last days for the restoration of his people, as he has spoken by the mouth of his prophets, and for the gathering of his saints to stand upon Mount Zion, in which shall be the city of New Jerusalem. Which city shall be built, beginning at the temple lot, which is appointed by the finger of the Lord, in the western boundaries of the State of Missouri, and dedicated by the hand of Joseph Smith, Jun., and others with whom the Lord was well pleased. Verily this is the word of the Lord, that the city New Jerusalem shall be built by the gathering of the saints, beginning at this place, even the place of the temple, which temple shall be reared in this generation. For verily this generation shall not all pass away until an house shall be built unto the Lord, and a cloud shall rest upon it, which cloud shall be even the glory of the Lord, which shall fill the house. (Doctrine and Covenants 84:2–5)

> Therefore, as I said concerning the sons of Moses for the sons of Moses and also the sons of Aaron shall offer an acceptable offering and sacrifice in the house of the Lord, which house shall be built unto the Lord in this generation, upon the consecrated spot as I have appointed. (Doctrine and Covenants 84:31)

The Mormon's New Jerusalem and temple was not built in Missouri and definitely not in that generation, which came and went many years ago.

The Mormons have an extensive seven-volume set of the *History of the Church* which was originally *History of Joseph Smith*. It includes Smith's writings and subsequent comments by Smith's secretaries and scribes (those close to him). Then it picks up with Mormon historians once Joseph Smith died. In volume 2, we read:

> President Smith then stated that the meeting had been called, because God had commanded it; and it was made known to him by vision and by the Holy Spirit. He then gave a relation of some of the circumstances attending us while journeying to Zion – our trials, sufferings; and said God had not designed all this for nothing, but He had it in remembrance yet; and it was the will of God that those who went to Zion, with a determination to lay down their lives, if necessary, should be ordained to the ministry, and go forth to prune the vineyard for the last time, for the coming of the Lord, which was nigh – even fifty-six years should wind up the scene. (Joseph Smith, *History of the Church*, Vol. 2, p. 182)

So Smith claimed 56 years "should wind up the scene"—in other words, Jesus should have returned by now as this was stated in 1835 before Smith's death in 1844, but 1891, 56 years later, has come and gone.

Jehovah's Witnesses

The Watch Tower Society or Jehovah's Witnesses, who have claimed Charles Taze Russell as the continuous prophet, have had the most failed prophecies in modern times.

> 1889 True, it is expecting great things to claim, as we do, that within the coming twenty-six years, all present governments will be overthrown and dissolved.[25] 1889 Remember that the *forty years'* Jewish Harvest ended October, A.D. 69, and was followed by the complete overthrow of that nation; and that likewise the forty years of the Gospel age harvest will end October, 1914, and that likewise the overthrow of

25. Charles Russell, *Studies in the Scriptures*, Vol. 2, 1889, p. 98–99.

"Christendom," so-called, must be expected to immediately follow.[26] For just one sample of the Watch Tower Society's failed prophecies surrounding the year 1925, consider:

- In 1918, they write, "...and since other Scriptures definitely fix the fact that there will be a resurrection of Abraham, Isaac, Jacob and other faithful ones of old, and that these will have the first favor, we may expect 1925 to witness the return of these faithful men of Israel from the condition of death, being resurrected and fully restored to perfect humanity and made the visible, legal representatives of the new order of things on earth. ... Therefore we may confidently expect that 1925 will mark the return of Abraham, Isaac, Jacob and the faithful prophets of old, particularly those named by the Apostle in Hebrews chapter 11, to the condition of human perfection." (*Millions Now Living Will Never Die*, 1920, p. 88–90)
- In 1923 they write, "Our thought is, that 1925 is definitely settled by the Scriptures." (*Watch Tower*, April 1, 1923, p. 106)

Jehovah's Witnesses have failed to predict the end of the world on a variety of occasions, including 1908, 1914, 1918, 1925, 1941, and 1975. Their prophecies continue to fail.

Other False Prophets

And there are many more false prophets, some who were specific and wrong,[27] and others, who were so vague that they become meaningless. Here are just a few failed prophecies in our modern times (including some secular predictions):

- Harold Camping falsely prophesied that the end of the age would be in 1994 in his book *1994*. When that didn't happen, he revised his date and said it would occur on May 21, 2011. When that too failed, he moved it ahead to October of the same year. That came and went.

26. Charles Russell, *Studies in the Scriptures*, Vol. 2, 1889, p. 245.
27. E.g., (1) Herbert Armstrong (too many to list), (2) Ellen G. White (claimed to have a vision of heaven in *Early Writings*, p. 32, where she saw the Temple in the Holy City, but the Bible says there is no Temple in heaven in Revelation 21:22), and (3) Jim Jones (who murdered his flock).

- Charles Darwin predicted the so-called Caucasians would exterminate all other "races" within the not very distant future (measured by centuries at the most).[28] Now we know there is only one race – the human race. The Bible has always taught we all come from Adam and are therefore one race, a fact which has now been confirmed by genetics. Darwin's prediction, based on his warped understanding of the human family, never happened.
- Clarence Larkin believed the Second Coming would commence no later than A.D. 2000 with a rapture occurring seven years before.[29]
- Edgar Whisenant's book *88 Reasons Why the Rapture Will Be in 1988* also failed.
- Pat Robertson falsely predicted that Mitt Romney would be elected the President of the United States in 2012, have two terms, and the economy would turn around under his presidency. He attributed this directly to the Lord. Instead, Romney, a Mormon, lost the election.
- William Miller (father of Millerites and Adventism) predicted that Christ would return on March 21, 1844, and then later said October 22, 1844. Clearly, this didn't happen.
- Al Gore (evolutionist) predicted in January of 2006 that the global warming point of no return for a true planetary emergency would occur in just 10 years. A decade came and went. This is a failed prophecy.
- Stephen Hawking, Richard Dawkins, Neil deGrasse Tyson, and others have predicted we will find aliens. We're all still waiting!
- Nigel Barber claimed atheism would defeat religion by the year 2038.[30] (Of course, atheism *is* a religion so that would be impossible!)

This is just a taste of the false prophets who have come and gone. Even in the New Testament they dealt with false prophets (e.g., Bar-Jesus in Acts 13:6[31])

28. Charles Darwin, *The Descent of Man,* 2nd Edition, A.L. Burt, New York, 1874, p. 178.
29. Clarence Larkin, *Dispensational Truth*, Rev. Clarence Larkin Est. Publisher, Philadelphia, Pennsylvania, 1918, p. 16.
30. Nigel Barber, "Atheism to Defeat Religion by 2038," *Huffington Post* Science, June 5, 2012, http://www.huffingtonpost.com/nigel-barber/atheism-to-defeat-religion-by-2038_b_1565108.html.
31. Now when they had gone through the island to Paphos, they found a certain sorcerer, a false prophet, a Jew whose name *was* Bar-Jesus. (Acts 13:6)

and likewise the early church also had to deal with them (e.g., Marcionism).[32]

These examples all illustrates this point: if you can't trust the prophecies of alleged prophets, why trust their other proclamations? Jesus wisely said to Nicodemus:

> *If I have told you earthly things and you do not believe, how will you believe if I tell you heavenly things?* (John 3:12)

Conclusion

Since these alleged holy books and prophets are not from the perfect God, who are they from? They are from fallible, deceived, mankind and may also be from deceiving spirits and demons as the Bible reveals:

> *Now the Spirit expressly says that in latter times some will depart from the faith, giving heed to deceiving spirits and doctrines of demons, speaking lies in hypocrisy, having their own conscience seared with a hot iron, forbidding to marry, and commanding to abstain from foods which God created to be received with thanksgiving by those who believe and know the truth.* (1 Timothy 4:1–3, NKJV)

The Bible warns that false philosophies will turn people from Christ (Colossians 2:8[33]), therefore Christians must be on the alert, standing firm on the Bible and not being swayed by man's word (1 Corinthians 15:58[34]; 2 Thessalonians 2:15[35]).

You only have two options: place your faith in the perfect, all-knowing God who has always been there, or trust the words of imperfect, fallible mankind. The Bible, God's holy Word, is superior to all other alleged holy

32. A cult in the second century that taught the heretic Marcion of Sinope should be trusted. Essentially, Marcion wanted the Old Testament to be thrown out as Scripture. He also threw out most of the New Testament with the exception of 10 of Paul's letters.
33. Beware lest anyone cheat you through philosophy and empty deceit, according to the tradition of men, according to the basic principles of the world, and not according to Christ. (Colossians 2:8)
34. Therefore, my beloved brethren, be steadfast, immovable, always abounding in the work of the Lord, knowing that your labor is not in vain in the Lord. (1 Corinthians 15:58)
35. Therefore, brethren, stand fast and hold the traditions which you were taught, whether by word or our epistle. (2 Thessalonians 2:15)

books. God will never be wrong or contradict Himself. So start with the Bible and build your faith on its teachings, which is pleasing to God.

We have no need for new revelation after the Bible—God's Word is final and complete:

> *Beloved, while I was very diligent to write to you concerning our common salvation, I found it necessary to write to you exhorting you to contend earnestly for the faith which was once for all delivered to the saints.* (Jude 1:3)

The Seriousness of Sin – Breaking God's Law

What Is Sin?

What is sin? How we can be saved from the wrath of a perfect, holy God that our sins deserve?

Sin is breaking God's law. We've all broken God's perfect law.[1] We sinned in our ancestor, Adam[2] (this is called original sin), and we continue to sin. We sin by commission and omission. Sins of commission are *doing what God forbids* and sins of omission are *not being or doing what God requires.*

In our culture today—sadly even in some of the church— sin is ignored, celebrated, or even encouraged. Some proclaim that certain sins—especially sexual sins—are not sins and others go so far as to say you're sinning if you call out sin as defined in the Bible! Others will use their own preferences, or conscience issues, to define what sin is, calling things that the Bible doesn't say are sins, sin.

Be careful what you call sin and what you say is not a sin. God's Word, not our opinions, traditions, likes/dislikes, or culture, defines sin.

1. For all have sinned and fall short of the glory of God. (Romans 3:23)
2. For as in Adam all die, even so in Christ all shall be made alive. (1 Corinthians 15:22)

God Defines Sin Through the Law

Since God, as the ultimate standard for right and wrong, alone defines sin we must know God's law. It's this perfect law that tells us what sin is.

> *But we know that the law is good if one uses it lawfully, knowing this: that the law is not made for a righteous person, but for the lawless and insubordinate, for the ungodly and for sinners, for the unholy and profane, for murderers of fathers and murderers of mothers, for manslayers, for fornicators, for sodomites, for kidnappers, for liars, for perjurers, and if there is any other thing that is contrary to sound doctrine, according to the glorious gospel of the blessed God which was committed to my trust.* (1 Timothy 1:8–11)

Does God have the power to change His laws to man at different times and for different circumstances?

Yes (and, by the way, this does not affect the unchanging *nature* of God). Here's an example: God originally only permitted man and the animals to eat plants (Genesis 1:29[3]). After the global Flood, God also gave meat as food (Genesis 9:3[4]). At the time of Moses, the Israelites were only permitted to eat meat from clean animals. But under the New Covenant[5] all foods have been made clean—which is not a problem for an all-powerful God. So we, as Christians, can eat all foods.

Or here's another example. From Adam's first sin until Christ people offered sacrifices to God to cover sin. Abel offered sacrifices (Genesis 4:4[6]), as did Noah (Genesis 8:20–21[7]), Abraham (e.g., Genesis 22:13[8]),

---

3. And God said, "See, I have given you every herb that yields seed which is on the face of all the earth, and every tree whose fruit yields seed; to you it shall be for food." (Genesis 1:29)
4. Every moving thing that lives shall be food for you. I have given you all things, even as the green herbs. (Genesis 9:3)
5. Because it does not enter his heart but his stomach, and is eliminated, thus purifying all foods? (Mark 7:19)

   And a voice spoke to him again the second time, "What God has cleansed you must not call common." (Acts 10:15)
6. Abel also brought of the firstborn of his flock and of their fat. And the LORD respected Abel and his offering. (Genesis 4:4)
7. Then Noah built an altar to the LORD, and took of every clean animal and of every clean bird, and offered burnt offerings on the altar. (Genesis 8:20–21)
8. Then Abraham lifted his eyes and looked, and there behind him was a ram caught in a thicket by its horns. So Abraham went and took the ram, and offered it up for a burnt offering instead of his son. (Genesis 22:13)

and the Israelites (repeatedly in obedience to God's specific commands). However, after Christ offered Himself as the ultimate Passover sacrifice (e.g., John 10:17–18[9]; Hebrews 9:28[10]), man no longer needed to sacrifice because Christ's sacrifice was sufficient once for all (Hebrews 10:10). This is why sacrifice is no longer required of man.

So there are cases where God, by His own power and authority, could and did change his laws. The key is using Scripture to see what God changed and when.

What Is the Punishment for Sin?

The punishment for the first man's sin and rebellion against God in the Garden of Eden was death (Genesis 2:17[11], 3:19[12]). Adam committed high treason against the Lord God who created him. Is sin serious? Yes.

The punishment from an infinite and eternal God would, by extension of God's very nature, be an infinite punishment that would go on forever (this is called the "second death" or "hell"). Man, being made in the image of an eternal God would receive this limitless wrath of God as an everlasting sentence. This is what hell is—an eternal punishment with the full wrath of God on man forever.

> *Beloved, do not avenge yourselves, but rather give place to wrath; for it is written, "Vengeance is Mine, I will repay," says the Lord.* (Romans 12:19)

Those animal sacrifices, starting in the Garden of Eden (Genesis 3:21) and continuing through Abel, Noah, Abraham, Isaac, Jacob, and the Israelites, were never going to be good enough—we're not related to the animals:

> *For it is not possible that the blood of bulls and goats could take away sins.* (Hebrews 10:4)

---

9. "Therefore My Father loves Me, because I lay down My life that I may take it again. "No one takes it from Me, but I lay it down of Myself. I have power to lay it down, and I have power to take it again. This command I have received from My Father." (John 10:17–18)
10. So Christ was offered once to bear the sins of many. To those who eagerly wait for Him He will appear a second time, apart from sin, for salvation. (Hebrews 9:28)
11. But of the tree of the knowledge of good and evil you shall not eat, for in the day that you eat of it you shall surely die. (Genesis 2:17)
12. In the sweat of your face you shall eat bread till you return to the ground, for out of it you were taken; for dust you are, and to dust you shall return. (Genesis 3:19)

Animals are not infinite or eternal. The best they could offer was a temporary covering for sin. These sacrifices, and the repetition of them, were a symbol, pointing to what we really needed: an infinite sacrifice that could take the infinite punishment from our infinite Creator.

Can Ceasing to Sin Save You?

If you stop sinning (if such a thing were even possible!) or start doing more good deeds, will that save you from God's wrath? No, God, being perfectly holy, must punish sin. And God, being perfectly just, must enact justice.

We have all sinned (Romans 3:23[13]) and have all committed high treason against God with even just one sin (breaking just one of God's laws). For "original sin" alone—our sin in Adam—we rightfully deserve God's infinite wrath!

You may think that is unfair of God, to punish us for what Adam did. But, because we were all "in Adam" when he, as the patriarch head of the human race, committed that sin, each of our lives was wrapped up in his when he rebelled. We see this concept elsewhere in Genesis. Levi was Abraham's great-grandson. Yet the Bible says that Levi was in the body of his ancestor Abraham when he paid tithes to Melchizedek.

> *Even Levi, who receives tithes, paid tithes through Abraham, so to speak, for he was still in the loins of his father when Melchizedek met him.* (Hebrews 7:9–10)

When Adam sinned, we all sinned because all of our lives were in Adam when he committed that sin. And we continue to sin. Even if it were possible to cease sinning, we would still need to be punished for the sins we already committed. So how is it that anyone could possibly be saved? (Don't worry—there's good news!)

The Good News!

We have a big problem—and there's nothing we can do about it. But all of those blood sacrifices in the Old Testament point us to the only solution to our problem: the only one even capable of taking that infinite and eternal punishment for us, the only one who would love and care enough for

13. For all have sinned and fall short of the glory of God. (Romans 3:23)

us to do such a thing, and the only one who is in a position of power to do anything about it: God Himself.

Yes, the very One whom we sinned against is the very One who stepped into history to save us from the sin problem we caused.

You see, God is love, and He is perfect love. The nature of God is Triune—there are three *persons* of the one Triune God. The love between those three persons (the Father, the Son, and the Holy Spirit) is of perfect essence. By this love, the Father sent His Son Jesus Christ to be sacrificed in our place and to take on Himself the infinite punishment we deserve for our sin. The Father enacted the punishment, and the Son endured it on the Cross—perfect justice for sin accomplished through the Son taking the full wrath of the Father upon Himself on our behalf (Isaiah 53).

Jesus Christ, the Son of God, took on flesh and became a man. He lived a perfect life, keeping the law without sin. It pleased God to punish Christ,[14] and this satisfied the wrath of God once for all by Christ's eternal nature. Then God raised Jesus up from the grave, defeating sin and death as He crushed the head of the serpent.

When we believe in Jesus Christ's work on the Cross and His death, burial, and Resurrection, we are saved. As a result of our salvation, we should *want* to turn from our sin in repentance and, by the power of God's Spirit dwelling in us, be obedient to Christ's commands.

Christians don't do good works to try to "earn" salvation; we do good works because we love Christ (John 14:15[15]). When people believe on Him, Christ's righteousness is transferred (imputed) to them so that they are now seen as spotless before the Father. Salvation is a gift of God, not by works, but by Christ's work on the Cross.

> *For by grace you have been saved through faith, and that not of yourselves; it is the gift of God, not of works, lest anyone should boast.* (Ephesians 2:8–9)

> *For God so loved the world that He gave His only begotten Son, that whoever believes in Him should not perish*

14. Yet it pleased the LORD to bruise Him; He has put Him to grief. When You make His soul an offering for sin, He shall see His seed, He shall prolong His days, And the pleasure of the LORD shall prosper in His hand. (Isaiah 53:10)
15. If you love Me, keep My commandments. (John 14:15)

but have everlasting life. For God did not send His Son into the world to condemn the world, but that the world through Him might be saved. He who believes in Him is not condemned; but he who does not believe is condemned already, because he has not believed in the name of the only begotten Son of God. (John 3:16–18)

Salvation is being saved from the wrath of God by His very grace that He bestowed on us. But it is so much more than that. It is experiencing the goodness of our loving God forever. We are made in the image of an eternal God, and we get to experience that great and eternal being forever.

But as it is written: "Eye has not seen, nor ear heard, nor have entered into the heart of man, the things which God has prepared for those who love Him." (1 Corinthians 2:9)

Conclusion

Will we one day sin in heaven and fall from God's grace? No. In the same way that the first Adam led us into sin, so Christ, the Last Adam, led us out of sin. And when Christ returns and consummates a perfect new heaven and new earth, Christ will forever be our head. We will never fall into sin again because Christ our eternal head *is* God and He cannot sin. We can rest assured that eternal life means everlasting life without the fear of falling back into sin.

Nevertheless, on this side of heaven, Christians still sin and sometimes still think wrongly (we are all in the process of being sanctified but a true Christian, despite their sin, will bear fruit in keeping with their repentance[16]). And when someone calls something sin that isn't sin, or refuses to call sin what it is, that shows an ignorance of God's Word or an elevation of *their own thoughts* above God's Word. But it's a dangerous position to attempt what God alone has the authority to do. But, praise the Lord, when we do sin we have an advocate in Jesus[17] and God promises, when we confess our sins, to forgive us in Christ.[18] Sin is indeed serious. But don't miss the best part! What God did to solve the sin problem is so

16. Therefore bear fruits worthy of repentance. (Matthew 3:8)
17. My little children, these things I write to you, so that you may not sin. And if anyone sins, we have an Advocate with the Father, Jesus Christ the righteous. (1 John 2:1)
18. If we confess our sins, He is faithful and just to forgive us our sins and to cleanse us from all unrighteousness. (1 John 1:9)

much more. When you are in Christ, there is a joy and peace of knowing that God's wrath no longer abides on you. The "sting of death" is taken away, and you can rest assured that your salvation is forever in Christ. May the Lord Jesus receive the eternal honor and glory. Amen.

Glossary of Terms

Agnosticism: a religion that claims you cannot know if God exists or not.

Agreeable fallacy: agree because you do it yourself.

AIP: acronym for critique that stands for arbitrary, inconsistent, and preconditions.

Ambiguity fallacy: vague, general words.

Appeal to fear: trying to get people to do something or else there may be consequences that you don't want to happen.

Appeal to pity: trying to get you to do something out of pity.

Appeal to progression: trying to influence through the construct of progress.

Appeal to technology: trying to influence via the latest thing.

Appeal to tradition: trying to influence due to tradition or age.

Apologetics: to give a logical defense of the Christian faith.

Arbitrary: nothing of substance behind an argument like unreasonable whims, blind opinions, or unjustified choices.

Atheism: a religion built on the idea of claiming to "know" there is no God.

Attack the person fallacy: attacking the person, not the point.

Authority test: Does the idea/statement/presupposition that I am confronted with have man as the ultimate authority or the God of the Bible as the ultimate authority?

Bandwagon: pressuring because many others are doing it.

Begging the question fallacy: using itself to prove itself in an arbitrary sense.

Behavioral inconsistency: preaching one thing but living another way.

By force fallacy: making everyone think it is the truth by force and power.

Carbon-14 (C14): has a relatively short half-life of around 5,700 years, and it decays into nitrogen.

Carnellian presuppositional method: The best worldview is the most coherent.

Circular reasoning: is considered valid in logic and reasoning, with two kinds being vicious (bad) and virtuous (good).

Clarkian presuppositional method: The best worldview is the most logical.

Classical apologetics: assumes that autonomous rational thought (i.e., based on man's reasoning alone) is the "absolute standard" regarding philosophical debates.

Composition fallacy: using a statement to judge the whole, using some small thing to illustrate the whole thing.

Compound questions fallacy: using one or more questions to try to trick the opponent.

Confirmatory: a confirmation of what we expect to find.

Contrary to fact conditional error fallacy: alters historical facts and draws conclusions from them.

Contrary to premise fallacy: self-contradicting right from the start.

Converse fallacy of accident: come up with science rules and laws based on accidents.

Cumulative case: not itself a "model," but instead, uses several previously discussed models—like a smorgasbord—in conjunction together to argue for the existence of God.

Deductive arguments: conclusion is said to be definitely true if the premises are true.

Disrespect fallacy: condemning an argument because of where/how/who began it.

Double standard fallacy: saying one thing and doing another or applying something unequally, depending on who is making the case.

Either-or fallacy: making someone choose between two things when there are other possible options.

Emotive language fallacy: words lacking defined language—usually biased to upset someone.

Empiricism: true knowledge only comes from the senses.

Enthymemes: when a premise or conclusion is unstated.

Equivocation fallacy: using more than one sense of the word, tone, paraphrasing, multiple interpretations of a word, or incorrect assumption about a word.

Evidential apologetics: starts with autonomous rational thought as the "absolute standard" and that when people evaluate evidence (e.g., miracles in the Bible, or any sort of historical evidence and scientific evidence), they might come to the right conclusion regarding Christianity in general.

Exigency: giving time limits to influence you.

Failed step fallacy: conclusions do not follow the logic.

Fallacy: when an argument violates sound logic or sound reasoning.

Fallacy of accident: apply a general rule because of an obscure event.

Fallacy of division: dividing things that are not divisible or using the whole to judge one statement (opposite of composition).

Fallacy fallacy: just because there is a fallacy doesn't mean the conclusion must be wrong—sometimes a conclusion can still be right even when falsely-argued.

False analogy fallacy: using a similar argument to argue the point regardless of different circumstances.

False cause fallacy: because something randomly happened by accident doesn't mean it always will or just because something happened before something else doesn't mean it caused the other.

Faulty appeal to authority fallacy: no basis or power behind an argument because they are a lesser authority.

Fideism: means "by faith alone."

Figure of speech fallacy: misusing idioms.

Genetic error fallacy: determining if it is true by who is saying it now.

Guilt by association fallacy: falsely trying to link one group or set of ideas to another known group or known set of ideas that is false.

Hasty generalizations: generalizing about a class or group based on a small sample.

Humanism: a religion that essentially places humans on top and everything else.

Ignorance fallacy: assuming something is true because one is ignorant to the subject.

Ignorant conjecture: arbitrary because it has no real weight behind the belief.

Inductive arguments: conclusion is said to be likely or probably the case, but not definitely.

Insufficient evidence fallacy: using inadequate evidence to jump to a conclusion.

Intelligibility: refers to the quality of being clear and easy to understand.

Irrelevance fallacy: introducing and/or jumping to disproving the wrong point.

Law of non-contradiction: something cannot be "A" and "Not A" in the same relationship and at the same time.

Logic: the study of correct and incorrect reasoning.

Materialism: belief that only matter/energy exist within the natural universe (i.e., no spiritual realm).

Misinterpretation of a statement fallacy: not just a word—violations of context.

Misplaced authority fallacy: asking an expert to give an opinion about something he is not an expert in.

Naturalism: the religious perspective that nature (i.e., the universe) is all that exists.

No true Scotsman fallacy: defining a word or argument in such a biased way to protect the argument from rebuttal.

Offense fallacy: something is wrong merely because someone is offended by it.

Omnibenevolence: loving and kindness.

Omnibonitas: all-goodness.

Omniiustitia: all-just/justice.

Omniperfectio: all-perfect.

Omnipotent: all-powerful.

Omnipresent: all-present; existing everywhere, all at once.

Omnisanctitas: all-holiness.

Omnisapientia: all-wisdom.

Omniscient: all-knowing.

Omniveritas: all-truth.

Omnivita: all-life-giving/sustaining.

Pathetic fallacy: a type of reification fallacy reflecting human feelings, actions, or emotions through inanimate objects.

Pity fallacy: pity or looking for sympathy.

Polytheistic: believe in many gods, including the possibility that people are gods as well.

Potent: means "power" or "force," from the Latin word potentia.

Preconditions of intelligibility: those things that must be predicated as true upfront for something to make sense.

Prejudice/masses fallacy: appeal to the masses, prejudice of groups.

Premises: certain accepted ideas or basic information.

Presuppositional apologetics: God and His Word are the absolute and only standards of morality, logic, uniformity in nature, dignity, etc., and the Bible provides the only basis for a worldview that makes knowledge possible.

Presuppositional tension: looking at the basis for an argument to see if there is consistency for it.

Pretended neutrality fallacy: trying to take a supposed stance of "neutrality."

Probabilistic: not certain or absolute.

Propaganda: very commonly and successfully used information to get people to act on or believe something often presented in a biased or misleading way.

Personification fallacy: a type of reification fallacy that treats animals as though they have human characteristics.

Propositions: chain of statements and premises that are assigned a truth value (true or false), and conclusions.

Rationalism: reason is the test of knowledge.

Reductio ad absurdum: reducing the argument to absurdity by where it leads.

Reformed epistemology: instead of concluding that God exists, we can have an innate sense of His existence when we experience creation; therefore, because of this, the claim is that God exists.

Reification fallacy: treating abstract concepts, objects, and events of nature as real things with human characteristics.

Repetition: repeating something so many times that people begin to believe it regardless of the facts.

Respect fallacy: giving airs to truth due to prestige, respect, etc.

Schaefferian presuppositional method: The best worldview will give the best answers to life.

The sheep hear His voice method: holds that the existence of God is known to us because of John 10:27.

Slippery slope fallacy: absurdly extrapolating.

Snob appeal: trying to get people to think they are better than everyone else.

Strawman fallacy: when someone attacks or refutes a distorted view of what their opponent believes instead of their actual position.

Supernaturalism: where supernatural beings, like the God of the Bible and His angels can exist.

TAG method (transcendental argument for the existence of God): not an argument per se but rather the basis for where all argumentation can begin and be sustained.

Transcendental apologetics: starts with God and His Word as the foundational starting point.

Transfer: trying to transfer a thought of one thing/person to another thing/person.

Triune God: God reveals Himself as a plurality in unity, God, the Father, God, the Son, and God the Holy Spirit.

Vicious abstraction fallacy: changing the argument to something else to try to prove the other point.

Index